# A Practical Guide to
# SELF-SUFFICIENCY

### Terry Bridge

CHARTWELL
BOOKS, INC.

Published in 2011 by
**CHARTWELL BOOKS, INC.**
A division of BOOK SALES, INC.
276 Fifth Avenue
Suite 206
New York
NY 10001
USA

**Copyright © 2011 Regency
House Publishing Limited**
Unit P1 Watermill Industrial Estate
Aspenden Road
Buntingford
Hertfordshire SG9 9JS
United Kingdom

For all editorial enquiries, please contact
Regency House Publishing at
**www.regencyhousepublishing.com**

ISBN-13: 978-0-7858-2791-7

Printed in China

This book is intended for those fortunate
enough to have a little land at their disposal
and wish to put it to better use, perhaps to
provide food for the family while creating a
greener, more ecologically-friendly
environment. It does not contain expert
advice; it is intended merely to encourage
and inspire and to give some idea as to what
self-sufficiency is all about.

# A Practical Guide to
# SELF-SUFFICIENCY

# CONTENTS

CHAPTER ONE
**SELF-SUFFICIENCY AS A WAY OF LIFE**
6

CHAPTER TWO
**SETTING UP & GETTING STARTED**
18

CHAPTER THREE
**GROWING YOUR OWN PRODUCE**
38

CHAPTER FOUR
**KEEPING ANIMALS**
104

CHAPTER FIVE
**KEEPING BEES**
170

CHAPTER SIX
**WILD FOODS**
186

CHAPTER SEVEN
**SELF-SUFFICIENCY IN THE  HOME**
196

CHAPTER EIGHT
**PRESERVING FOODS**
214

CHAPTER NINE
**SPINNING**
226

CHAPTER TEN
**FARMERS' MARKETS**
234

CHAPTER ELEVEN
**MILK PRODUCTS**
240

**INDEX**
250

# CHAPTER ONE

# SELF-SUFFICIENCY AS A WAY OF LIFE

*Today, as many of us are becoming more eco-conscious and concerned with 'carbon footprints' and other pressing environmental issues, thoughts are turning to ways of sustaining a simpler, greener way of life in which we are producers rather then consumers. For many, complete self-sufficiency may be an unattainable dream, but small ways can be found in which to provide for some of our own basic needs.*

The aim of self-sufficiency is to achieve a sustainable, healthy and happy lifestyle while respecting the land, wasting next to nothing and reducing the call on the Earth's dwindling resources. Those who aspire to this enviable lifestyle may also attempt to reduce their individual carbon footprints by making changes in their use of transportation, the amount of energy consumed, and in the kinds of food they eat. They may also

conduct their lives in ways that are consistent with sustainability while preserving a natural balance that is respectful of mankind's symbiotic relationship with the Earth's natural ecology and cycles. The practice and general philosophy of ecological living is therefore closely linked with the principles of sustainable development.

The time when we grew our own food crops, reared animals for meat and other by-products, and bartered for goods and services has become a thing of the distant past. In recent years, however, many have begun to question how our food is produced, particularly where intensive farming methods are involved, and a certain nostalgia has developed for a time when we were more self-reliant and could make important choices for ourselves.

Carbon footprints may be altered for the good by reducing the amount of energy used to produce our food. We can also seek to check the encroachment of man-made chemicals into our lives and concentrate on rearing animals in more humane and compassionate ways. There is a bonus

here, for it is generally accepted that home-grown food is fresher and tastes better than that which has been mass-produced, is fully traceable, and will be cheaper in the long run, making the argument for self-sufficiency a compelling one. Most of us, however, will be unable to adopt this lifestyle in its fullest sense but must be content with a few vegetables grown in an urban plot.

As the way we live becomes increasingly more urban and land in short supply, remember that even a city balcony can be used to great effect to grow a few tomatoes, strawberries and herbs, while a city allotment can produce a good supply of seasonal vegetables for those with more time and enthusiasm. Not everyone wishes to abandon the city for a rural ideal, but for those who do, a move to the country and the purchase of some land can be an exciting prospect indeed, allowing us to reconnect with the planet while fulfilling a rural dream.

OPPOSITE: A few chickens will supply all the fresh eggs you need, while a surplus can be given to neighbours and friends.

ABOVE: An apple orchard in full bloom. Carefully stored, apples will last for ages and windfalls can also be used to make jellies, chutneys and wines.

Growing your own food produces an enormous sense of achievement and allows you to develop skills and knowledge that will remain with you

are contributing to global warming. Many scientists and environmentalists have, therefore, urged a global switch to renewable energy, which derives from the sun or from processes set in motion by the sun. These energy forms include direct use of solar power along with windmills, hydroelectric dams, ocean thermal energy systems, and biomass (solid wood, methane gas or liquid fuels). It will therefore become more and more cost-effective to provide your own renewable energy, whether it be in the form of a wind turbine or solar panels which will eventually pay for themselves.

Self-sufficiency goes hand-in-hand with the organic movement that began

for life. Self-sufficiency, as a lifestyle choice, is an education in itself, as far as children are concerned, teaching them where their food comes from and the bearing it has on health. They will also realize the value of food, not to waste it, and the wisdom of preserving the environment for future generations.

Acid rain is clearly the result of the use of fossil fuels, and most climatologists also believe these fuels

ABOVE: Piglets eventually grow to be large animals which need a good deal of space.

RIGHT: Keeping bees is a fascinating and rewarding experience although some initial specialist advice would not go amiss.

chemicals. Today, we see wholefood stores as integral parts of the grocery shopping market.

Farming organically is not only about reducing the use of chemicals but also about managing the land by means of good husbandry to ensure that the soil is kept well-structured and in good condition. The land should be kept well-drained and well-fertilized using organic compounds. Grazing land should be managed so that it does not become overgrazed or allowed to become overgrown, while the careful choice and rotation of livestock on the land is of paramount importance.

It is advisable to get the rest of your family or friends involved before

LEFT & BELOW: Growing your own fruit and herbs is not only cost-effective but also a way of providing fresh, tasty additions to your diet.

taking the road to self-sufficiency, as there will be a lot of work to do and a job shared is a job halved. You will also need to be realistic concerning the amount of time you have at your disposal, for the need to keep a full- or part-time job to supplement your income can be frustrating when you would rather be working on your land. Remember that keeping animals can be something of a tie; they can never be left to their own devices and finding someone to cover for you in an emergency is an almost impossible task.

in the early 1900s in response to the shift towards synthetic nitrogen fertilizers and pesticides in the early days of industrial agriculture. It lay dormant for many years, kept alive by a relatively small group of ecologically-minded farmers. In recent years, however, environmental awareness has driven demand and conversion to organic farming, which some governments, including the European Union, have begun to support through agricultural subsidy reform. Organic production and marketing have grown at a fast pace. The term 'organic' can broadly be described as food grown without the assistance of man-made

# SELF-SUFFICIENCY AS A WAY OF LIFE

It is important, at this point, to consider any initial financial outlays that may be necessary. It may be that you already have some land at your disposal, but it is more likely that you will need to find a more suitable location for your new venture. From basic gardening tools to stables and chicken sheds – essential equipment can be expensive – and the need to buy them can play havoc with your finances.

There are alternatives, should you have reservations about making a complete change to your lifestyle. You might consider taking an allotment or becoming a member of an urban farm or community garden, which would allow you to reap the benefits of partial self-sufficiency without making the ultimate commitment; it could also act as a stepping-stone towards making a final decision at a later date.

Out-sourcing tasks can be expensive, which could well make some of your end-product financially unviable. It may be that one family member is good at mechanics and the other at dealing with animals, so the more free talent you have at your disposal the better. Your own physical stamina is also an important factor: working the land involves hard work

ABOVE RIGHT & RIGHT: Even city dwellers can be self-sufficient to a certain extent by utilizing balconies and window sills to grow a few vegetables and herbs.

and long hours. If you have a medical condition, or possibly a back problem, you will have to consider the kinds of crops you grow as some will need more attention than others.

A challenging issue that will have to be faced is your attitude towards raising animals for meat; these animals must be viewed dispassionately, not as pets, in that you will eventually have to take them for slaughter. If this is an issue that troubles you, then a course in animal husbandry to educate yourself as to what exactly is involved may prove invaluable. If you come to the conclusion that rearing animals for food is not for you, then you can always

concentrate on raising crops and leaving meat production to those more suited to the task.

## BALCONIES AND WINDOW SILLS: MICRO SELF-SUFFICIENCY

There is still scope for a degree of self-sufficiency in an urban environment – even a balcony can yield great rewards. Initially it may seem that little can be achieved, but a small patch can, in reality, be suitably planted to provide worthwhile results. Sunny window sills are great for tomatoes, and hanging baskets can be used to grow trailing strawberry plants and herbs.

Some outside space and there are other opportunities; city farms or allotments can be utilized to grow more ambitious crops and foraging for free food from hedgerows and wild spaces is another possibility. When foraging, however, make sure that endangered or poisonous species are left strictly alone and that anything taken has not been growing in contaminated soil or been polluted by passing traffic.

An environmentally-friendly philosophy can also extend to the home. Use natural fibres for soft furnishings, pay attention to how well the building is insulated, and make use of grey water (waste water) whenever possible.

## SMALL SPACES

Even a house with a very small garden presents opportunities for self-

sufficiency. Fruit and vegetables can be grown and a few chickens or even bees can also be kept, provided there is sufficient land to support them. Animals require clean, draft-free accommodation with good ventilation and natural lighting. Foodstuffs must also be kept in dry, clean conditions, and waste material in areas where harmful pests cannot colonize it.

Almost all areas of a small garden may be utilized. As well as ordinary vegetable beds, raised beds and containers are useful where space is at a premium. It also makes environmental sense to plant species that attract native insects and birds; this way you are helping both the natural world and yourself at the same time.

Even a small backyard can produce a good yield of fruit and vegetables, while at the same time attracting bees and other beneficial insects.

## COMMUNITY GARDENS AND ALLOTMENT PLOTS

Allotments and community gardens were originally introduced into the United States and Britain in the 19th century to provide the poor with land on which to grow their own food.

Today, however, they are regarded as a way of getting back to nature and growing food that is fresher, tastier and more nutritious than anything that can be bought. This valuable resource is more popular than ever and demand is so high that it is often necessary to get

BELOW: Many local authorities supply land which can be rented cheaply for growing food.

OPPOSITE: This urban farm is provided by the City of Chicago for the use of the local community.

on a waiting list with the hope that a plot will eventually become available.

Check local rules and regulations to avoid the disappointment that you may be unable to take your dog with you, or even your children if they are under a certain age. There are often regulations concerning the use of water, pesticides and herbicides, and there can be restrictions regarding the types of plants that can be grown. Note also that the keeping of livestock, such as chickens, is often banned. In an ideal world you will be provided with a shed or lock-up in which you can store all your tools and equipment.

There are also benefits from living close to your plot, as a long journey time to and fro can act as something of a discouragement.

## CITY FARMS AND COMMUNITY PROJECTS

City farms are community-run projects in urban areas which involve people working with animals and plants. They aim to improve community relationships and offer an awareness of agriculture and farming to people living in built-up areas.

They vary in size from small plots on housing schemes to larger farms that occupy a number of acres. It is estimated that more than three million people visit city farms each year and around half a million work on them as volunteers. Although some city farms

have paid employees, most rely heavily on volunteer labour, and some are run by volunteers alone. Others operate in partnerships with local authorities. City farms provide a great introduction for anyone with aspirations towards self-sufficiency. There are many skills to be acquired, including milking techniques, handling livestock, feeding them, cleaning and general animal husbandry. Valuable tips and advice can also be had concerning fruit- and vegetable-growing.

## LARGE GARDENS

A house with a large garden can be converted into a small hobby farm, with vegetables, poultry and even a few

beehives, while an acre of land will support a couple of pigs or goats. A hobby farm is cultivated, primarily, for the sheer pleasure of growing food for the family and a few friends, with no thought of making a financial gain.

The large garden is a pathway towards realizing a part-time, self-sufficient life in that it is big enough to provide a family with seasonal produce, but not so large that it means working on it full-time. It also offers the best of both worlds in that a a city career can be followed while devoting evenings and weekends to the garden tasks in hand.

A large vegetable garden typically includes a compost heap and several plots or divided areas of land intended to grow one or two types of plant in each plot. It is usually located to the rear of a property, and many families have such kitchen and vegetable gardens in which they grow a significant amount of their own food.

With money now in short supply, and with the increasing interest in organic and sustainable living, many people are turning to vegetable-growing to supplement their family's diet. Food grown in the backyard consumes little if any fuel as far as transport or maintenance are concerned, and the grower will know exactly what has gone into producing it. If the garden is large enough, a greenhouse or polytunnel is a great way of extending the growing season and will allow a greater range of produce to be grown. It may be necessary, however, to check if planning permission is required before erecting them. Yields will also be greatly increased, in the event of which you may consider selling produce that is surplus to requirements at your local farmers' market.

Keeping animals is another possibility, but you will need to check that it is legal to do so, as local laws often prevent animals from being kept in gardens. If, however, you find that it is permitted, and your neighbours have no objections, a few animals such as chickens, rabbits, goats, ducks and geese will provide you with eggs and meat. Make sure the animals have plenty of space and that they are correctly fed and kept clean.

If you have the space, it may also be beneficial to install a wind turbine or solar panels to help generate the electricity to power your property.

## SMALLHOLDINGS

A smallholding is a piece of land with adjacent living quarters for the smallholder and accommodation for farm animals. It is on a smaller scale than a farm but larger than an allotment. It is often established for the breeding of farm animals on an organic basis on free-range pastures. The smallholder may alternatively concentrate on the growing of vegetables by various traditional

OPPOSITE: A large backyard is all that is needed in which to grow fruit and vegetables and keep a few chickens.

RIGHT: The smalholder will benefit from a large barn in which to store tools, even animals and their feed, during the harsher winter months.

methods or in a more modern way using plastic covers, polytunnelling or cloches for fast growth.

Generally, a smallholding offers the smallholder a means of achieving self-sufficiency when it comes to providing for his and his family's own needs, which he may be able to supplement by selling surplus produce at farmers' markets. Permanent retail facilities are often included.

A smallholding usually consists of land that has been subdivided into areas for fruit trees, shrubs or various types of vegetables. In this type of establishment, once the initial layout and investment (in plants, trees, shrubs, etc.) has been made, only the replanting of annual vegetables, the maintenance of perennials and the minimum of weeding of the area needs to be undertaken.

All kinds of animals may be kept on a smallholding and even larger animals, such as pigs and cattle, are a possibility. It is vital, however, not to overcrowd the land as overgrazing can become a big problem. If you are keeping grazing animals, make sure you have sufficient space to grow grass to make silage and hay to provide food for them in winter.

If managed correctly, and with attention paid to all aspects of self-sufficiency, a smallholding should be able to provide year-round produce that is enough to sustain an average family.

## FARMS

The decision to opt for a small farm rather than a smallholding is a difficult one and, generally speaking, must be a carefully costed out, commercial venture. It is assumed that the farm will be a full-time occupation and will therefore be the farmer's only source of income. In addition to the initial purchase of the land, the necessary machinery will also be required and is likely to be a considerable outlay in financial terms.

New farm buildings may well be required and everything, down to the last detail, must be considered to avoid disappointment or even disaster later on.

With self-sufficiency in mind the farm should be fully integrated with its surrounding environment so that plants and animals can be raised with as little outside intervention as possible. Waste products must be processed so that manure and compost can be recycled and returned to improve the soil.

Taking on a small farm is a big commitment and it may take many years for it to pay for itself.

# CHAPTER TWO

# SETTING UP & GETTING STARTED

*O*nce all aspects of achieving self-sufficiency have been considered, as discussed in Chapter One, you will be ready to take the next step.

Be careful that your initial enthusiasm does not blinker you when assessing all the problems you may encounter along your way. It is a very big financial step that you are taking, with an initial large investment. Make sure there is enough money to take you through the first year or so, for you will be producing very little during this time. For many, this may well prove an impossibility, so it may be necessary to maintain a day job during the early stages of the venture.

The set-up costs, including the purchase of the land and property, are very high, while equipment, machinery, animal housing, veterinary products etc. are very expensive. Approach the whole plan as if you were embarking on a new business venture and remember to budget for the unexpected. If you intend

Take special care when choosing land for your new venture, seeking as much expert advice as possible.

to borrow money from a bank to get started, you will need to demonstrate that you can afford the repayments on the loan and that sufficient income from the venture can be generated to keep you going.

Before purchasing land, remember to do your research; it is wise to use a conveyancer who has had experience in agricultural property and who has been informed exactly of your requirements.

At this point you should check to see if there are any rights of way across your intended land as this could pose a problem in the future. Get all the advice you can, preferably from experts in the field. Issues regarding planning permission are particularly challenging, so it must not be assumed that it is easy to get. For this reason it is often wise to buy land for which the vendor has already applied and been granted

planning permission for the buildings you require. Planning laws vary from country to country and from place to place, so it is important to check the local regulations that may be in force. Some buildings, such as field shelters, polytunnels, sheds and greenhouses, may not be regarded as permanent structures, making them exempt from planning permission in some areas, but do not make any assumptions. You may also have to get planning permission to change the use of the land, particularly if you want to use some of it for an additional business venture.

Ideally, the type of land you should be looking for is well-drained, flat, fertile and well-situated, but

ABOVE: Smallholders and farmers should always consider living on site, particularly if animals are involved.

RIGHT: Check with local authorities that you can erect such structures as field shelters and polytunnels before buying land.

compromises may have to be made. If there are problems connected with the land in question, e.g., it may be a little steep or wet in places, then it should be priced accordingly.

Your land and farm buildings will need services. Water and electricity can be very expensive to install, so it is a great bonus if they are already in situ.

Accommodation for you and your family on site is always the best option and allows you to keep an eye on your property and tend to your plants and animals without having to travel far. Some will be looking for a house suitable for the whole family and might even consider extending it, for which planning permission would be required. There are others, however, who would be happy living in a mobile home or other temporary accommodation until they can build a home of their own. As with the land, the presence of electricity, water and possibly a gas

supply are important factors, as installing them will add substantially to the costs. A telephone line is also an important consideration: in some rural areas high-speed internet access is still unavailable and, without it, online services will be unavailable.

Many factors will influence your choice of location, some of which may be personal, but if you intend to run your new venture as a business, you will have to consider your customer base. Should you decide on a remote, rural location, then you may have to become more internet-based, setting up a website from which to sell your

produce. If you find it impossible to generate enough income, it may be that other family members may wish to take a job in the local community. Proximity to a local town will greatly improve their chances of getting employment.

Self-sufficiency is a lifestyle choice worth striving for, but like everything worthwhile requires dedication and hard work. Not only do you have to be practical and well-organized, you will also need to develop new talents. First and foremost, you will be running a business, so you will have to grapple with accounts, banking, budgets and stock-taking. You will need good

BELOW: Farm equipment is vital and usually expensive; make sure you have made good provision for purchasing it.

OPPOSITE: Working with horses can be hugely rewarding, but advice and tuition must be sought unless you have experience in handling them.

secretarial skills, be able to type well, be computer-literate and learn to maintain accurate records, while marketing skills will also play a necessary part. Whether you sell via the internet, mail order or at local markets, you will have to price and package your wares in such a way that

they can compete in the marketplace. You can do your own market research or, if extra tuition is required, you can attend a local college for a part-time course in the subject.

Many of the jobs necessary for self-sufficiency can ideally be split between family members. The more practical, physically stronger members may concentrate on building and mechanical tasks, while other tasks, such as paperwork, cooking and feeding the animals can be designated to younger or older family members.

If horses are to be kept and used for working the land, then a lot of specialist know-how and experience will be required, as it is impossible to start from scratch without the backup of an experienced horseman. Horses are intelligent and rewarding animals to own, so with help and advice on hand it is well worth considering them.

Where the farming side is concerned, the smallholder will have to be accomplished in many tasks, including animal husbandry, arable farming and vegetable-growing, to name but a few, plus the ability to turn produce into saleable or edible goods. Being good at cooking, brewing, pickling, preserving and arts and crafts are all skills that connect well with the self-sufficient way of life.

Training for Self-Sufficiency
Many excellent practical courses are available where most aspects of self-sufficiency are covered, and some courses attract diplomas or other qualifications that may become useful in the future. There is never a real substitute for practical experience, however; seek out volunteer groups that run community or city farms where it is possible to find other like-minded people willing to offer hands-on, practical advice that will increase confidence. It is always a good idea to join organizations which publish regular magazines and pamphlets on all aspects of the subject; these will help

you keep abreast with the ever-changing technologies of organic and sustainable farming. The public library is often a necessary port of call, where books and other publications are usually available free of charge.

Join a farming organization. Often, they not only offer subsidized insurance policies, loans and other agriculture-related services but they also publish monthly magazines. If it is your intention to specialize in a particular breed of animal, or indeed a rare breed, then join the appropriate breed society for that animal. This will provide you

with advice on breeding, feeding, health and the general welfare of the type of animal concerned.

## Land Management
### The soil, drainage and water supply
Soil consists of layers (soil horizons) of mineral constituents of variable thicknesses which differ from the parent materials in their morphological, physical, chemical and mineralogical characteristics. It is composed of particles of broken rock that have been altered by chemical and environmental processes that include weathering and erosion. Soil differs from its parent rock due to interactions between the lithosphere, hydrosphere, atmosphere and the biosphere. It is a mixture of mineral and organic constituents that are in solid, gaseous and aqueous states.

Soil is essential for agriculture, where it serves as the primary nutrient base for plants; as demonstrated by hydroponics, however, it is not essential to plant growth if the soil-contained nutrients can be dissolved in a solution. The types of soil used in agriculture (among other things, such as the purported level of moisture in the soil) vary with respect to the species of plants that are cultivated.

Soil resources are critical to the environment as well as to food and fibre production. Soil delivers minerals and water to plants, absorbs rainwater and releases it later, thus preventing

floods and drought. Soil cleans the water as it percolates. It is the habitat for many organisms: in fact, the major part of known and unknown biodiversity is in the soil in the form of invertebrates (earthworms, woodlice, millipedes, centipedes, snails, slugs, mites, springtails, enchytraeids, nematodes, protists), bacteria, archaea, fungi and algae, and most organisms that live above ground have part of them (plants) or spend part of their life cycle (insects) below ground. Biodiversities above and below ground are tightly interconnected, making soil protection of paramount importance

BELOW; Good-quality, well-maintained soil and an adequate water supply are vital for the growing of healthy crops.

OPPOSITE: Drainage ditches are simple to construct and are an easy and efficient solution to the problem of removing surface water.

where any restoration or conservation plans are concerned.

In terms of soil texture, soil type usually refers to the different sizes of mineral particles in a particular sample. Soil is made up in part of finely ground

rock particles, grouped according to size as sand, silt and clay. Each size plays a significantly different role. For example, the largest particles, sand, determine aeration and drainage characteristics, while the tiniest, sub-microscopic clay particles are chemically active, binding themselves with water and plant nutrients. The ratio of these sizes determines soil type, i.e., clay, loam, clay-loam, silt-loam and so on.

In addition to the mineral composition of soil, humus (organic material) also plays a crucial part in soil characteristics and fertility for plant life. Soil may be mixed with larger aggregates, such as pebbles or gravel. Not all types of soil, for example, pure clay, are permeable.

*There are many recognized soil classifications, both international and national.*

**Fertile soil has the following properties:**
• It is rich in nutrients necessary for basic plant nutrition, including nitrogen, phosphorus and potassium.
• It contains sufficient minerals (trace elements) for plant nutrition, including boron, chlorine, cobalt, copper, iron, manganese, magnesium, molybdenum, sulphur and zinc.
• It contains organic matter that improves soil structure and soil moisture retention.
• Soil pH is in the range 6.0 to 6.8 for most plants, but some prefer acid or alkaline conditions.
• Good soil structure creates well-drained soil, but some soils are wetter (as for producing rice) or drier (as for producing plants susceptible to fungi or rot) such as agave.
• A range of micro-organisms that support plant growth.
• Often contains large amounts of topsoil.

In lands used for agriculture and other human activities, fertile soil typically arises from the use of soil conservation practices. In order to become self-sufficient, good practices in soil management are essential.

Keeping the soil well-drained is essential to good farming. While plants need moisture to grow successfully, they can be hindered by excess water. If land is being used for grazing, waterlogged land will quickly become poached, making the number of animals kept per acre that much more limited.

Ditches are a simple way of capturing run-off, while under-soil drainage is more expensive. This is where clay or plastic pipes are inserted beneath the soil to take excess water away from the surface.

Of concern to many farmers, in that it may reduce plant growth, is soil compaction caused by heavy field traffic, which may clearly be observed in wheel ruts. Compaction is usually caused by working the soil when it is too wet, and clay soils are more likely to become impacted than sandy ones.

# SETTING UP AND GETTING STARTED

## Management of Grazing Land

Grazing generally describes a type of predation in which a herbivore feeds on plants (such as grasses) and also on other multicellular autotrophs (such as algae). Grazing differs from true predation because the organism being eaten is not generally killed; it differs from parasitism as the two organisms do not live together, nor is the grazer necessarily so limited in what it can eat.

Many small selective herbivores follow larger grazers, which skim off the topmost, tough growth of plants, exposing tender shoots. For terrestrial animals, grazing is normally distinguished from browsing in that grazing is eating grass, or other low vegetation, and browsing is eating woody twigs and leaves from trees and shrubs.

Grazing is important in agriculture, in which domestic livestock are used to

BELOW: Taking good care of grazing land pays dividends in the long run, as if will provide good, nutrious food for your animals.

OPPOSITE: Wildflowers and herbs add variety to your animals' diet.

convert grass and other forage into meat, milk and other products.

In the 19th century, grazing techniques were virtually non-existent.

Pastures would be grazed for long periods of time, with no rest in between. This led to overgrazing, which was detrimental to the land, wildlife, and livestock producers. Today, ranchers and farmers have developed grazing systems to help improve the forage production for livestock while still being beneficial to the land.

The two major types of grazing management are controlled and continuous. With continuous grazing, the livestock has free selection of forage, while with controlled grazing the producer regulates forage availability and quality.

Seasonal grazing incorporates grazing animals on a particular area for only part of the year. This allows the land that is not being grazed to rest and allows for new forage to grow.

Rotational grazing involves dividing the range into several pastures and then grazing each in sequence

throughout the grazing period. Utilizing rotational grazing can improve livestock distribution while incorporating rest periods for new forage.

Rest rotation grazing divides the range into at least four pastures. One pasture remains rested throughout the year and grazing is rotated throughout the residual pastures. This grazing system can be especially beneficial when using sensitive grasses that require time for rest and re-growth.

Deferred rotation involves at least two pastures with one not grazed until after seed-set. By using deferred rotation, grasses can achieve maximum growth during the period when no grazing occurs.

Be careful not to overstock your grazing land: too many animals will overgraze the land which can possibly lead to welfare issues.

Grazing animals drink a lot of water, particularly when it is hot. It is essential, therefore, to have a piped supply through to a water trough on a free-draining site that will help prevent poaching.

Grassland should be regularly topped and harrowed to keep it in good condition. Grazing animals usually favour some plants more than others and the good grasses will get eaten down hard, leaving ragged weeds, such as dock and nettles, to become rampant if left to their own devices for any length of time.

## Hay

Hay is grass, legumes or other herbaceous plants that have been cut, dried and stored for use as animal fodder, particularly for grazing livestock such as cattle, horses, goats and sheep. Hay is also fed to pets such as rabbits and guinea pigs. Pigs may be fed hay, but they do not digest it as efficiently as more fully herbivorous animals.

Hay is fed when or where there is not enough pasture or rangeland on which to graze an animal, when grazing is unavailable due to weather (such as during the winter) or when lush pasture by itself is too rich for the health of the animal. It is also fed during times when an animal is unable to access pasture, such as when animals are kept in stables or barns.

Commonly used plants for hay include mixtures of grasses such as ryegrass, timothy, brome, fescue, bermuda grass, orchard grass and other species, depending on region. Hay may also include legumes, such as alfalfa (lucerne) and clovers (red, white and subterranean). Other pasture forbs are also sometimes a part of the mix, though other than legumes, which are ideally cut pre-bloom, forbs are not necessarily desirable. Certain forbs are toxic to some animals.

It is the leaf and seed material in the hay that determines its quality. Farmers try to harvest hay at the point when the seedheads are not quite ripe and the leaf is at its maximum when the grass is mowed in the field. The cut material is allowed to dry so that the bulk of the moisture is removed but the leafy material is still robust enough to be picked up from the ground by machinery and processed into storage bales, stacks or pits.

Hay is very sensitive to weather conditions, particularly when it is harvested. In drought conditions, both seed and leaf production are stunted, making hay that has a high ratio of dry coarse stems that have very low nutritional values. If the weather is too wet, the cut hay may spoil in the field before it can be baled. The hay may also develop rot and mould after being baled, creating the potential for toxins to form in the feed, which could make animals sick. It also has to be stored in a manner that will prevent it from getting wet.

Hay can be raked into rows as it is cut, then turned periodically to dry,

OPPOSITE & BELOW: Good grass produces cheap food for your livestock and hay to feed them during the leaner winter months.

# SETTING UP AND GETTING STARTED

particularly if a modern swather is used. Or, especially with older equipment or methods, the hay is cut and allowed to lie spread out in the field until it is dry, then raked into rows for processing into bales afterwards.

During the drying period, which may take several days, the process is usually hastened by turning the cut hay over with a hay rake or spreading it out using a tedder. If it rains while the hay is drying, turning the windrow will also allow it to dry faster. Turning the hay too often or too roughly, however, can also cause drying leaf-matter to fall off, reducing the nutrients available to the animals. Drying can also be hastened by mechanized processes, such as the use of a hay conditioner or by spraying chemicals onto the hay to speed evaporation of moisture. These, however, are more expensive techniques that are not in general use except in areas where there is a combination of modern technology, highly-priced hay, and too much rain for hay to dry properly.

Once hay has been cut, dried and raked into windrows, it is usually gathered into bales or bundles, then hauled to a central location for storage. In some places, depending on

BELOW: Once made, hay must not be allowed to get wet but stored in a barn to ensure there is a good supply of fodder for the winter months. This barn would benefit from doors or plastic sheeting being hung to cover up the entrance.

OPPOSITE: Harvesting hay for silage.

geography, region, climate and culture, hay is gathered loose and stacked without being baled first.

Hay must be fully dried when baled and kept dry in storage. If hay is baled while too moist, or becomes wet while in storage, there is a significant risk of spontaneous combustion. Hay stored outside must be stacked in such a way that moisture contact is minimal, while some stacks are arranged in such a way that the hay itself 'sheds' water as it falls. Other methods of stacking use the first layers or bales of hay as a cover to protect the remainder.

To exclude moisture completely, outside haystacks can also be covered by tarpaulins, and many round bales are partially wrapped in plastic as part of the baling process. Hay is also stored under a roof when resources permit. It is frequently placed inside sheds or stacked inside barns.

Care must also be taken that hay is never exposed to any source of heat or flame, as dry hay, and the dust it produces, are highly flammable.

## Silage

Silage is fermented, high-moisture fodder that can be fed to ruminants (cud-chewing animals like cattle and sheep) or used as a biofuel feedstock for anaerobic digesters. It is fermented and stored in a process called ensiling or silaging, and is usually made from grass crops, including corn (maize) or sorghum or other cereals using not only the grain but the entire green plant.

Silage is made either by placing cut green vegetation in a silo, or by piling it in a large heap covered with plastic sheeting, or by wrapping large bales in plastic film.

Silage must be firmly packed to minimize the oxygen content or it will spoil. It goes through four major stages in a silo:

• Presealing, which, after the first few

days after filling a silo, enables some respiration and some dry matter (DM) loss, but stops

- Fermentation, which occurs over a few weeks; pH drops; there is more DM loss, but hemicellulose is broken down; aerobic respiration stops
- Infiltration, which enables some oxygen infiltration, allowing for limited microbial respiration; available carbohydrates (CHOs) are lost as heat and gas
- Emptying, which exposes surface, causing additional loss; rate of loss increases.

## Haylage

Haylage is a name for high dry-matter silage of around 45–75 per cent, while horse haylage is usually 55–75 per cent dry matter, made in small or larger bales. The handling of wrapped bales is most often done with some type of gripper, that squeezes the plastic-covered bale between two metal parts to avoid puncturing the plastic.

Simple fixed versions are available for round bales which are made of two shaped pipes or tubes spaced apart to slide beneath the sides of the bale, but when lifted will not allow the bale to slip through. Often used on the tractor rear three-point linkage, they incorporate a trip-tipping mechanism which can flip the bales on the thickest plastic layers over onto the flat side/end for storage.

## Animal Housing, Machinery, Tools and Storage

A barn is an agricultural building used for storage and as a covered workplace. It may sometimes be used to house livestock or to store farm vehicles and equipment. Barns are most commonly found on farms or former farms.

Older barns were usually built from lumber sawn from timber on the farm, although stone barns were sometimes built in areas where stone was a cheaper building material.

BELOW: Storing equipment in a barn will prolong its life.

OPPOSITE: This old timber barn, as well as being useful, is rather more attractive than its modern counterpart.

Modern barns are more typically steel buildings. Prior to the 1900s, most barns were timber-framed (also known as post-and-beam) forming very strong structures that would withstand storms

and heavy loads of animal feed. From about 1900 to 1940 in the northern USA, many large dairy barns were built which commonly had gambrel or hip roofs to maximize the size of the hayloft above the dairy roof, and have become associated with the popular image of a dairy farm. The barns that were common in the wheatbelt held large numbers of pulling horses, such as Clydesdales or Percherons. These large wooden barns, especially when filled with hay, could spectacularly

LEFT: This old barn, with two grain silos close by, has been brought back into the 21st century with a new roof and modern extension.

BELOW: Single-storey barns are often used as animal shelters during the winter months.

catch fire and were usually total losses for the farmers. With the advent of balers it became possible to store hay and straw outdoors in stacks surrounded by a ploughed fireguard.

# SETTING UP AND GETTING STARTED

Many barns in the northern United States are painted red with a white trim, a possible reason for this being that ferric oxide, which is used to create red paint, was the cheapest and most readily available chemical in New England and adjacent areas. Another reason may be that ferric oxide acts as a preservative and that painting a barn with it would help protect the structure.

With the rise of tractors following the Second World War, many barns were demolished or replaced with modern Quonset huts made of plywood or galvanized steel. Beef ranches and dairies began building smaller loftless barns, often of Quonset or of steel walls on a treated wood frame (old telephone or power poles). By the 1960s it was found that cattle receive sufficient shelter from trees or wind fences – usually wooden slabs 20 per cent open.

In older-style barns, the upper area was used to store hay and sometimes grain. This is called the mow (rhymes with cow) or the hayloft. A large door at the top of the ends of the barn could be opened up so that hay could be put into the loft. The hay was hoisted into the barn by a system containing pulleys and a trolley that ran along a track attached to the top ridge of the barn. Trap doors in the floor allowed animal feed to be dropped into the mangers for the animals.

A farm often has pens of varying shapes and sizes used to shelter large and smaller animals. The pens used to shelter large animals are known as stalls and are usually located on the lower floor. Other common areas or features of a typical barn include:

- Tack room (where bridles, saddles, etc. are kept) – often set up as a break room
- Feed room, where animal feed is stored – not typically part of a modern barn where feed bales are piled in a stackyard
- Drive bay, a wide corridor for animals or machinery
- Silo, where fermented grain or hay (called ensilage or haylage) is stored
- Milkhouse for dairy barns; an attached structure where the milk is collected and stored prior to shipment
- Grain (soy, corn, etc.) bin for dairy barns, found in the mow and usually made of wood with a chute to the ground floor providing access to the grain, making it easier to feed the cows
- Modern barns often contain an indoor corral with a squeeze chute for giving veterinary treatment to sick animals

## Fences and Boundaries

It is a good idea to fence the perimeter of your land with a good-quality fence-line as this will discourage intruders as well as unwanted wildlife. (Some fences are specially designed to keep deer or

OPPOSITE ABOVE: Post-and-rail is ideal for a boundary fence, being very robust, easy to repair and safe for animals.

OPPOSITE BELOW: Stock fence is a good option for smaller animals such as sheep. It must be kept tight and well-maintained If combined with barbed wire.

other large animals out.) The fence should be safe, not only for your own stock but also for wildlife. It should also be robust enough to keep your animals in. Cattle, horses and other stock can be quite destructive, so your external boundary should be regularly inspected and maintained to prevent animals from escaping. If your animals were to get onto a highway or onto your neighbours' crops it could well spell disaster in human or financial terms. Insurance must be taken out to protect you from the results of your stock straying off your land.

When deciding on a piece of land to purchase, be sure to find out who owns the boundary fence between you and your neighbour. Fences and parallel ditches can be very expensive to maintain and, should the responsibility be yours, you will have to factor in any potential costs.

Rabbits, deer or foxes may pose particular problems. If they are likely to become a potential nuisance, by eating your crops or attacking your chickens, you will have to put in

Provided that your external boundaries have been made secure, there are a wide variety of internal fences from which to choose and which range in cost.

Hedges have many plus points: they are wildlife-friendly, providing valuable corridors; they look great, providing shade or shelter for stock; and they deter intruders. For extra security hedges are best combined with post-and-rail or post-and-wire fencing. Hedges require regular trimming and must also be checked for weak areas that will need re-planting. Trimming should only be carried out at times when birds have finished nesting. This is often a legal requirement.

additional fencing. Keeping rabbits out is always a battle: small-mesh rabbit netting must be sunk into the ground up to a depth of 12 inches. The netting also needs to be fairly high (up to 3 feet) as rabbits are good jumpers. .

Foxes are particularly determined when it comes to getting food, especially when they have young. A combination of electric fencing and poultry netting can be partially effective, but some foxes will always find a way in.

Keeping deer out is always going to be expensive as they are quite large; therefore your fence needs to be high enough and will benefit from being electrified, too.

in the corner of a field will have a funnel effect and this will help you to guide your animals through. Gates can usually be bought ready-made in metal or in wood, both of which work well, although the metal ones are lighter and will need less maintenance.

## Wildlife

All open land is beneficial to wildlife, and even an urban micro-holding can be vital to the ecology of the area. Before even beginning to plan the layout of your smallholding, garden or farm, take some time, not only to plan for crops and livestock, but also to consider the wildlife of the area. It may be that your land has some pre-existing features that lend themselves to helping birds, plants and animals survive. Sometimes it is better to be slow to tidy things away; that fallen log or that marshy area may be far better left strictly alone. Try to find some information regarding the ecology of your area (a public library is a good place for this) and try to discover the plants, insects and other wildlife that you should be encouraging (or discouraging).

It is common knowledge that bees are in decline, so plants that attract bees and other pollinating insects should be nurtured or planted. It is often better, if you are fortunate enough to have some traditional meadowland, to leave it well alone, or at least maintain it in the traditional way; overdraining the land

Rivers and streams do not provide the best kind of barrier for animals, but may help to restrict movement. Lowland sheep tend not to cross water, but other animals, such as horses, will happily cross a stream. Like hedges, it is safer that rivers and streams are bordered with post-and-wire or post-and-rail fencing.

Post-and-rail and post-and-wire can also be combined with netting to keep animals confined. Both can be further protected with a strand or two of electric tape to prevent animals from rubbing or chewing the fences. Barbed

wire is suitable in certain circumstances but must be meticulously maintained and kept taut. It must never been used near horses.

## Gateways

The siting of gateways is of great importance. Areas which stay wet in winter do not make good gateways, so try to find some higher, drier areas on which to site them. If wet ground is unavoidable, however, the chosen area can be dug out and hardcore added to help with the drainage. If you are likely to be herding your animals, a gateway or adding unnecessary fertilizers can be detrimental to land and wildlife alike.

Wooded areas may not attract great financial rewards, but they are vital as far as wildlife is concerned, and add biodiversity, or a variety of life, to the land. Ponds, and water in general, are of utmost importance in attracting wildlife to an area and must be protected. If you have some spare space, try constructing a pond, but be careful to fence it to prevent small children and vulnerable animals from falling in. Remember that each of us has a duty to ensure a diverse and thriving natural environment for future generations.

It is possible to increase the ecological value of land by planting native hedges, trees and plants. Protect your wildlife areas and leave places where rough grass flourishes to its own devices. Do not overtrim hedges and try to limit or preferably stop using herbicides and pesticides altogether.

While wildlife is generally welcome in our gardens and farms, it may be necessary, at some stage, to view certain visitors as pests. If you are becoming overrun by foxes, rabbits, weeds or

OPPOSITE: An example of a badly-fenced field. The loose posts are joined together with baggy barbed wire which is not only unattractive but dangerous to animals and people.

ABOVE RIGHT: Galvanized metal gates last longer than wood and require little maintenance.

other nuisances, try to use non-toxic controls. Keep chickens securely housed, and if you have worries where rodents are concerned, ensure that feedstuffs are kept in vermin-proof containers. To discourage birds, use scarecrows or other bird-frighteners. Surplus rabbits and pigeons can be shot and used for food, but you must make sure you comply with gun-licensing laws and that you are qualified to handle firearms.

# CHAPTER THREE
## GROWING YOUR OWN PRODUCE

*Growing one's own vegetables is increasing in popularity. Not only is it an interesting and rewarding occupation, but the result is also fresher, better-tasting, and the vitamins and minerals contained within them have more chance of being preserved.*

Given the concerns surrounding climate change, reducing the time that our food takes to reach our tables will also serve to reduce any adverse effects on the environment. It has been estimated that the ingredients making up the average festive family meal could well clock up as many as 48,000 miles or twice the circumference of the Earth. These 'food miles' all contribute to our carbon footprints, which are the measure of the impact our activities are having on the environment, so as well as cutting down on the energy we use, growing vegetables for our own use is also a way of cutting down on global warming.

The cut flower market clocks up even greater mileages, which can be offset by growing some cutting flowers yourself, for example, in an area being left fallow as part of a crop-rotation

OPPOSITE & ABOVE: Growing your own food brings many benefits, both for you, the environment and for your family's health.

cycle. Alternatively, scatter a few flower seeds around and between vegetables, which will attract beneficial insects and in some cases repel pests, or place a few large flower pots at intervals throughout the plot.

Not all ground is suitable for growing food, and it is important to consider any previous activity which may have left a residue of contaminants. If the area has been used for burning rubbish, for example, there could well be dioxins present, which are the products of plastics combustion, and there may also be unsafe levels of heavy metals from paints and some printed materials.

To grow well, vegetables need to be suited to the local climate. They need an open position away from buildings and overhanging trees. The aspect of the site has a bearing on growth rates,

therefore the ideal spot would be flat and south-facing, although a gentle slope would be less likely to be affected by spring frosts, in that cold air flows downhill. Sloping sites, on the other hand, are rather more difficult to use, in which case the plot may be set across it. South-facing plots may need added watering in the hotter months to ensure the soil does not dry out.

Ideally, full sunlight is required for much of the day, but with adequate shelter from strong winds. The best windbreaks should have 50 per cent permeability to allow some of the wind to pass through. Plant hedging around large plots or use netting around smaller ones. When positioning your vegetables, place those that will grow taller where they will not cast shadows over the smaller ones. Try to plant sun-loving vegetables in south-facing positions and those that prefer shade facing north.

ABOVE: This plot has an excellent quality of soil. It is also in an open area which gets plenty of sunlight while benefiting from a shelter belt of trees.

OPPOSITE: As plots are dug over, weeds can be eliminated and organic matter added.

## Preparing the Site

It can be particularly daunting to be faced with a neglected piece of ground, usually infested with weeds. A good way to tackle the work is to divide it into four areas for rotating annual crops, plus one for more permanent planting with rhubarb, herbs and soft fruits. Crop rotation is important to reduce the build-up of pests and diseases in the soil. The various crops use up nutrients differently so soil can become depleted if the same ones are grown repeatedly in the same spot.

On restricted sites, or where there is a more relaxed attitude to growing, a system of polyculture can be followed where there is no formal division of beds. Permaculture is the development of ecosystems intended to be sustainable and self-sufficient, the position of crops being determined by the maturing and harvesting of the previous ones.

Make a path through the centre of the plot, wide enough to accommodate a wheelbarrow and edged with gravel boards or scaffolding planks. If the site is fairly level, landscape fabric can be used, which acts as a barrier between soil and the preferred top mulch, preventing soil migration and ensuring a clean, attractive surface. Then use more landscape fabric to make side paths running at right-angles to the main one, pinning it down with wire hoops or plastic pegs. These can be moved to accommodate different planting configurations and to make cultivation easier.

Paths will also reduce the amount or trampling on the beds, so they may not need to be dug over again, apart from some light forking, to turn in some manure. This forms the basis of the no-dig method of gardening, where the organic matter is scattered over the surface and becomes incorporated during planting and by the action of worms in the soil.

One of the problems with developing a plot from a weedy condition, or from pasture, is that there may be more pests than usual, such as leatherjackets and wireworms. These pests live on the roots of plants so that when the weeds are removed they will turn their attention to your crops instead. When cultivating the soil, destroy any pests you find, a task at which you will find the birds will help and even keep you company as you work. There will also be a reservoir of weed seeds which will take quite a few years to be depleted. Some can remain viable for over 20 years, but their numbers will eventually decline if they are not allowed to mature.

It is probably best to plant in rows running in a north–south direction, which gives maximum light and fewer shadows. Sheds or greenhouses, if they are to be included, should be placed at the

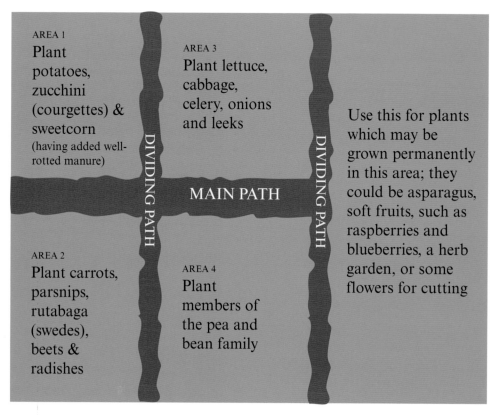

AREA 1
Plant potatoes, zucchini (courgettes) & sweetcorn (having added well-rotted manure)

AREA 3
Plant lettuce, cabbage, celery, onions and leeks

DIVIDING PATH

MAIN PATH

DIVIDING PATH

Use this for plants which may be grown permanently in this area; they could be asparagus, soft fruits, such as raspberries and blueberries, a herb garden, or some flowers for cutting

AREA 2
Plant carrots, parsnips, rutabaga (swedes), beets & radishes

AREA 4
Plant members of the pea and bean family

northern end to avoid shading of the plot. Should there be trees, large shrubs or a hedge nearby, their roots may extend into the plot, which will mean a loss of moisture and nutrients and the crops will suffer as a result. Smaller roots, which reach beyond the canopy, can be severed to lessen the problem, but larger supporting roots cannot, so you may need to choose another site. Once roots have been removed, however, a vertical barrier should prevent them from encroaching again.

The diagram (opposite) is a suggested layout for the first year. This will entail the addition of well-rotted manure or compost in Area 1, as potatoes require plenty of moisture and nutrition. (Zucchini/courgettes and sweetcorn are also gross feeders, so can be grown in this plot as well.) If the plot is large, this may be the only area tackled in the first year, with a little work done on the remainder. Cover any undeveloped areas with landscape fabric or old carpet laid upside-down to block out the light; this will kill existing weeds and prevent others from germinating, making it easier to cultivate later on. In subsequent years the rest of the plot will be subjected to double digging (see pages 44–45) as the crops rotate until they are back at the start after the fourth year, when the

A neat row of broccoli.

organic matter can be spread on the surface and incorporated with a digging fork. With a smaller plot, the whole can be dug over at once before dividing it into the different crop areas, at the same time incorporating organic matter into the relevant areas.

Most people would prefer to grow food without resorting to chemicals, but by suspending this good practice for a few weeks, the clearing of a new plot can be made less effortful by using a total weedkiller, which can be obtained from any garden store. This will destroy weeds and their roots, without leaving a residue in the soil, so that the ground can be used once clearing is complete. To facilitate total removal, leave the plot for a while to ensure that the more stubborn weeds are truly dead, repeating the procedure should they recover. This method may take longer than digging out the weeds, but it is more thorough and much easier on the back!

Once weeds have been removed, dig over the area with a fork, removing remaining weed roots and large stones. To add manure, remove a trench of soil to a depth of two spits (i.e. double the length of a spade's blade) at one end, moving it to just beyond the far end. Dig the manure into the bottom of this trench, being careful not to bring the subsoil up into the top layer, then turn the next row of spits on top of this. Repeat this along the area,

incorporating more manure as you go and covering it with the turned-over soil until the end is reached, when the soil from the first trench is used to fill in the last. This is the process known as double digging. If the ground has been cultivated before, or is easy to work, the double digging may be performed during the clearing operation.

This may seem like hard work, but the resulting bed will yield excellent crops for years. If you are not accustomed to this kind of work, then it should be tackled in small segments over a number of weeks when the weather is suitable. The rest of the plot may be treated in the same way later on or the following year, depending on its size and the gardener's energy level.

The following year use Area 2 for the potatoes, with the addition of manure. In the second year, Area 1 is used for other root vegetables, such as carrots, rutabaga/swedes, parsnips, beetroot and radishes, which do better in ground that has not been recently

OPPOSITE: Here, alfalfa (a leguminous plant) is being grown as a green manure, which will eventually be dug into the soil to add nutrients and organic matter. Alfalfa contains nitrogen-fixing, symbiotic bacteria in its root nodules that fix atmospheric nitrogen in a form that plants can readily use.

ABOVE: Raking in well-rotted manure.

manured. The potatoes move to Areas 3 and 4 in subsequent years, then start again in Area 1. This time the area does not require double digging as manure can be dug into the bottom of the trench in which the 'seed' potatoes are to be planted. Thus the four-year cycle begins again and proceeds in the same manner. (Crops to be planted in the rotation are as indicated in the diagram on page 42.) This is the ideal cropping arrangement, but preparation of the plot means that it may not become established for a few years.

A simpler rotation can be followed on a three-year cycle by including the potatoes with the root crops or leaving them out altogether if space does not permit. The crops are for the individual to choose, but those listed are the ones most commonly used.

The permanent planting areas can be placed at the northern end to reduce shading of the plot. The choice of crops depends on taste and the size of the area available, but are the ones which remain for a number of years, with strawberries lasting for about three years and asparagus for up to 20. Preparation is the same as for the rest of the plot. In subsequent years the area should be mulched with manure to keep weeds down, leaving the worms to work it into the soil. The non-cultivation or no-dig method of crop-growing uses this technique over the whole plot. The soil is not dug: instead, a thick mulch of compost or rotted manure is laid on the soil and the crops are planted through it. The initial preparation to clear the site is the same as before, as no amount of mulching will stop perennial weeds.

If there are periods when an area is not in production, for example, after harvesting a crop, it should be covered with a thick mulch of compost or with landscape fabric to prevent weeds from germinating; do not use plastic sheeting as it does not allow air in and the soil will become stagnant. The compost will be taken into the soil by worms, so

eliminating the need to dig to incorporate it the following spring.

Another use for fallow areas is to grow a green manure. This is an annual crop, such as mustard (spring or summer sowing) or alfalfa (late summer or autumn sowing). It will prevent soil erosion, smother weeds and improve the soil structure. Before the plants mature and still have plenty of sap, they are removed, left to wilt, then turned into the soil, roots and all, at least two to three weeks before re-planting, so that they are completely buried and left to break down, returning their nutrients to the soil. The soil structure is better maintained when it is being used with growing roots

keeping it open; a plot left barren, with nothing growing (even weeds), will soon become compacted and stagnant.

Other green manures, which can be grown in winter, are corn salad (lamb's lettuce) or fava (field or broad) beans, which have shallow roots and are easily incorporated. Keep to the principles of crop rotation by using varieties related to the harvested crop, for example, fava beans after peas/beans and mustard after brassicas. Phacelia is not related to any vegetable so can be used after any crop. Some of the seed sold for the purpose is used by commercial growers who use heavy machinery to incorporate the deeper roots and are not so suitable for garden use.

If the soil is not of a chalky nature it will tend to become acid as the calcium in the soil is leached out. Moreover, the addition of compost and manure tends to lower the pH (power of hydrogen). Consequently it may require the addition of lime from time to time as most vegetables grow best when the soil pH is between 5.5 and 7; this is because some of the nutrients become unavailable to plants beyond this range. It is preferable to do a pH test taking

| pH of soil | Sandy soil g/sq m | Loamy soil g/sq m | Clay soil g/sq m |
|---|---|---|---|
| 4.5 | 190 | 285 | 400 |
| 5.0 | 155 | 235 | 330 |
| 5.5 | 130 | 190 | 260 |
| 6.0 | 118 | 155 | 215 |

LEFT: Table showing the amount of lime in grams to be added per square metre to different soil types to achieve a pH of about 6–6.5.

OPPOSITE: Raised beds are ideal in small areas or where the existing soil is poor.

soil from several areas of the plot to work out the amount of lime to add to achieve this optimum level (see page 46).

Use ordinary lime (calcium carbonate), this being less caustic than quicklime (calcium oxide). Choose a calm day, marking out the area in $3ft^2$ strips, and sprinkle the lime evenly before digging it in. This is best done well before planting to avoid scorching roots and should not be applied at the same time as fertilizer or manure to avoid the loss of nitrogen; a chemical reaction causes ammonia to form, which is gaseous and escapes into the atmosphere. Late autumn or winter is traditionally the time when liming is carried out.

## Raised Beds

These have been in use for centuries and with good reason: they're not only better for all the vegetables you intend to grow but, being at a more comfortable level, where a gardener's anatomy is concerned, they reduce the aches and pains produced by kneeling or bending over. The beds can be built using wood, landscaping ties, decorative paving slabs or stone, with or without mortar (use your imagination where other materials are concerned). They should be no wider than 4ft so that plants growing in the middle can be reached from both sides. Raised beds exceeding 10ft (3m) in length will require additional stakes in the middle of the two long sides. This is

to keep them from bowing out under the weight of the soil should the sides be made of a flimsier material.

Raised garden beds are especially useful where space is limited, as the spacings between plants can be reduced. Building them is an easy task and they can also be purchased ready-made, there being a variety of quality modular beds available in kit form. Railway sleepers are also available and are excellent for this purpose.

Raised beds make it easier to introduce a rich and balanced growing medium. Fill them with the soil of your choice, then add plenty of well-rotted

manure or compost, maintaining and adding to this over time.

Soil conditions and types can be controlled more efficiently and may be varied from bed to bed. Moreover, the soil does not get compacted because it is not walked upon; remember, soil needs water and air to function and compaction robs it of both. Therefore soils that aren't compacted have a greater ability to hold plant-available water, form fewer clods, permit greater root growth and give higher plant yields as a result. Remember also that soil compaction has the potential to reduce yields by up to 50 per cent.

Other advantages of raised bed systems are:
- their tendency to drain away excess moisture better than ordinary garden beds
- the soil warms up quicker in the spring
- there is no need to dig beds over
- they are easier to keep weed- and pest-free
- frames for covers can easily be devised

## Tools and Equipment
You will need the correct tools for the job before starting work on your vegetable patch.

Using the correct tools for the job will not only make your work more pleasurable but also that much easier to perform. Tools should be cleaned and stored away in a dry place after every use.

**Spade**  Used to dig or loosen ground or to break up clumps of soil.
**Fork**  Used for loosening, lifting and turning over the soil.
**Hoe**  Used to weed and groom the soil around shallow-rooted plants, also to chop off annual weeds (perennial weeds must be dug up and removed) and plants at ground level. Can also be used to create narrow drills (furrows) and shallow trenches for planting seeds and

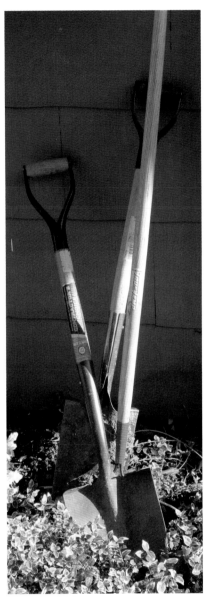

generally to dig and move soil (e.g. harvesting potatoes), and chop weeds, roots and crop residues.

**Rake** Used for removing waste material, such as dug-up weeds and stones, from the surface of the soil.

**Trowel** Used for breaking up soil, digging small holes – especially for planting and weeding – mixing in fertilizer or other additives, and transferring plants to pots.

**Wheebarrow** Used for moving soil, plants and other heavy garden objects from place to place.

## Greenhouses and Other Forms of Plant Protection

Prevailing climatic conditions affect the types of plants suitable for growing in different parts of the world; therefore, it makes sense to grow those that are most suited to your own particular environment. But where the serious

ABOVE: Cold frames are a good alternative to greenhouses where lack of space is an issue.

LEFT: A wheelbarrow is useful for shifting heavy loads about the garden.

OPPOSITE: Cloches can be used to extend the growing season, to raise seedlings, warm winter soil prior to planting and to 'harden off' plants. Cold frames and cloches also offer valuable extra space outside the crowded greenhouse.

gardener is concerned, the greenhouse is a more than useful addition, in that it permits a wider range of plants to be grown and also produces them earlier than the seasonal norm. If all you wish to do, however, is raise a few seedlings and cuttings, cloches, cold frames, conservatories and old-fashioned sun-porches may be sufficient for this purpose, although none of these offers quite the same amount of dedicated growing space as the true greenhouse.

## Shelter

One of the most important things a greenhouse can do is provide additional warmth and protection from the elements, and there is one particular aspect of this role which is often forgotten. While cold frames and mini-greenhouses manage this very effectively for plants, they provide little or no shelter for the gardener. Stealing a march, by bringing on plants during the cold, wet days of winter, is an attractive idea but not a particularly practical one without protection from the worst that winter has to offer.

But with a door to shut behind you, pottering about and checking how things are progressing suddenly becomes a more pleasant prospect, and with power, heat and light laid on, the useful hours that can be spent there can be greatly extended. While staying warm and dry is obviously relevant to us all, it may be of particular benefit

to the elderly or infirm. Nor is it only the gardener who gains; working with a cold frame open, the plants can get chilled, but in a greenhouse they are as well-protected as the gardener himself.

## Growing Opportunities

The greenhouse encourages us to grow at least some of our own food – also bedding plants. All manner of fruit and vegetables lend themselves to being grown even in unheated conditions – and the choice is not limited to tomatoes alone. Apart from the old greenhouse favourites, strawberries, chillies, peppers, eggplants (aubergines), peaches, nectarines, and even grapes, can all be raised successfully, provided suitable varieties are chosen, while the addition of some heat, during the colder months, makes even wider choices possible.

A final aspect, that tends to be overlooked, is the real contribution a greenhouse makes to the garden as a whole. Not only does it allow plants to be produced at a fraction of the cost of buying them, but there is also more satisfaction to be had from doing this, while a well-managed greenhouse can be regarded almost as an art form in itself.

πABOVE: A polytunnel is constructed from polythene tightly fixed over a metal frame. It does a similar job to a glass greenhouse but is cheaper and easier to erect.

OPPOSITE: Provided it is well-maintained, a greenhouse can be an attractive and useful addition to any backyard plot.

## Composting

No backyard farmer should be without some form of composter. Whether it be a heap in a corner or a more complicated arrangement, it is a place where suitable material can be left to rot down.

Composting is an excellent way to upcycle kitchen and garden waste into an extremely useful humus-like soil product, which permits the return to the soil of vital organic matter, nutrients, and bacteria in particular, that are vital to plant nutrition.

Composting biodegrades organic matter, and is performed by micro-organisms, mostly bacteria, but also by yeasts and fungi. The composting process produces an end-product that is dark, crumbly and sweet-smelling.

## Adding Organic Materials to a Compost Bin

Micro-organisms, such as bacteria and fungi, break down the soft material. This causes the compost to heat to around 140°F (60°C), which is the ideal temperature for micro-organisms to do

their work. The compost then cools to below 70°F, when small creatures, such as worms and insects, then break down the tougher material. The whole process usually takes about 3–9 months and results in a nutrient-rich material to return to your garden. The compost that is ready to use can be taken from the bottom of the pile, leaving the rest to complete the process.

## Compost Bins

Manufactured bins include plastic ones, turning units, hoops, cones and stacking bins. Home-made bins can be constructed from scrap wood, chicken wire, fencing or even old garbage cans with holes punched into their sides and base. A simple wooden bin can be made by creating a frame out of wood and attaching it to the ground by means of corner posts. It should have a capacity of about 50–80 gallons, and ideally have a lid to keep out rain. The bin should be placed in a sunny spot out of the wind. Improve drainage by first breaking up the soil beneath the compost bin.

ABOVE LEFT: Well-rotted compost can be returned to the soil, adding vital organic matter for plant nutrition.

LEFT: Composters may be bought ready-made but home-made versions do the job just as well. The wooden one was constructed from old pallets.

## Heirloom Vegetables

An heirloom vegetable is a cultivar that was commonly grown during earlier periods in human history, but which is not used in modern large-scale agriculture. Many heirloom vegetables have kept their traits through open pollination, while fruit varieties, such as apples, have been propagated over the centuries through grafts and cuttings. The trend for growing heirloom plants in gardens has been growing in popularity in the United States and Europe over the last decade.

Before the industrialization of agriculture, a much wider variety of plant foods was grown for human consumption. In modern agriculture in the industrialized world, most food crops are now grown in large, monocultural plots. In order to maximize consistency, few varieties of each type of crop are grown. These varieties are often selected for their productivity, their ability to withstand mechanical picking and cross-country shipping, and their tolerance to drought, frost or pesticides. Heirloom gardening is a reaction against this trend. In the some parts of the world, such plants are still widely grown, for example in the home gardens of South and South-East Asia.

Heirloom growers have different motivations. Some grow particular plants for their historical interest, while

others wish to increase the available gene pool for future generations or select heirloom plants because of their interest in traditional organic gardening. Many, however, simply wish to taste the different varieties of vegetables, or see whether or not they are capable of growing rare varieties.

LEFT: Growing historic plants may help preserve rare genetic varieties, such as this heirloom corn.

ABOVE: Only a few of the many kinds of potato are commercially grown, leaving these heirloom varieties to be grown by enthusiasts.

## Sowing and Planting

Certain seeds may require a prior treatment, before sowing, such as scarification, stratification, soaking or cleaning using cold or medium–hot water. Seeds can either be sown broadcast or in drills. Sowing broadcast means scattering the seeds on the surface of the soil, and sowing in drills means setting seeds in soil in orderly rows. Sowing in rows is particularly appropriate where vegetables are concerned and where many different kinds will be grown, each one, preferably, in a row of its own.

Before sowing seeds, the ground needs to be prepared by digging it over with a spade to make sure there are no large lumps of soil or stones, then raking over the surface to make a seedbed with a fine 'tilth', which is when the soil is sufficiently broken down into fine particles that will not impede the passage of the tiny seeds as they germinate and begin to push up through the surface of the soil.

Planting is simply putting an existing plant or bulb into soil, that is appropriate for the individual plant, to allow it to grow and develop. Make a hole in the soil where you wish to plant, then place the root ball of the

When the seedlings have developed leaves and strong roots, divide them up into single plants and re-plant them in trays or individual pots. Protect tender plants from frost.

plant into the hole, filling it in with soil. Using your hands, press the soil around the stem so that the root ball is firmly anchored, ensuring that the roots make good contact with the soil.

To transplant is to transfer seedlings, grown in a seedbed, to the actual site where the plants will be required to grow on. This not only toughens the plants but also stimulates growth.

**Drills** To sow in drills, dig over the soil, rake it, then mark out rows with a stick or the back of a hoe. Sow the seeds in the rows, then cover the seeds by raking the soil from the sides of the row over the drill. Water gently. Small seeds are usually sprinkled evenly along the row, while large seeds, such as peas or beans, can be sown singly a few inches apart. If the seedlings come up too thickly to allow the plants room to grow properly, then you will need to thin them out by removing the unwanted, weaker seedlings.

**Seedbeds** Specific areas where seeds are sown for germination. The area is preferably level and with a fine soil which helps the young plants to break through and makes it easy to lift them for planting out. The seedlings may be

These raised areas are used as seedbeds to produce seedlings that will later be transplanted into the main vegetable plot.

left to grow to adult plants in the seedbed, perhaps after thinning them to remove the weaker ones, or they may be moved elsewhere as young plants.

Growing Vegetables
Some of the following are not vegetables, in the true sense of the word, but most people would consider and use them as such.

## FAVA (BROAD) BEANS

Prepare the soil well in advance; it should have been well-dug and treated with manure the previous winter. Seeds are best sown outdoors in open ground, the usual time being from March to May, but if the climate is mild, the soil is well-drained and there is natural shelter, seeds may be sown in November. Sow beans 2 inches (5cm) deep, with 8in (20cm) between seeds, in rows 24in (60cm) apart. There should be no need to thin out the seedlings. Beans sown in the fall will be ready in 26 weeks, those spring-sown in about 14 weeks.

Alternatively, if a greenhouse, cold frame or cool window sill is available, it is possible to sow seeds in deep seed trays or modules. The seeds will take

about 14 days to germinate and should be ready to plant out in early March for harvesting in late May and June.

## GREEN & RED BEANS

The soil should be well-dug, slightly acid, moisture-retentive and well-manured. The seeds may be sown in April in protective cloches, or in late May or early June in open ground. Remove cloches in late May. Sow the seeds in drills 2in (5cm) deep, one bean every 4in (10cm) apart, with about 18in (45cm) between rows. Support the plants as they grow with short twigs or bean sticks, using longer canes or netting for climbing varieties. The beans will be ready for harvesting in 8–12 weeks.

ABOVE LEFT & LEFT: Fava (broad) beans.

ABOVE: Red or kidney beans.

## BEETS (BEETROOT)

Beets prefer an unshaded spot in a light sandy soil, the soil having been already limed if acid. The seeds may be sown outdoors in open ground or started off in 8-in (20-cm) pots. For an early crop (late May), sow the seeds in pots in February, keeping them above 55°F (13°C). From mid-April onwards, the seeds may be sown directly into a prepared seedbed. Continue to sow new batches of seed every month to extend the cropping period up to the end of June.

To speed germination, pre-soak the seeds in tepid water for 24 hours, sowing the seeds while they are still wet. The first seedlings should appear within 10–14 days. If originally sown in pots, plant out when the beets are about 4in (10cm) tall, hardening off the plants over two weeks; for early crops

plant them out initially under polythene or cloches. Allow 2in (5cm) between plants with 12in (30cm) between rows.

In open ground, sow two seeds together about 1in (2.5cm) deep, 2in (5cm) apart, with 12in (30cm) between rows. When the seedlings are about an inch high, thin out the weaker where both seeds have germinated, discarding the thinnings. Harvest 11–16 weeks after planting.

To store late-cropping beets, lift on a dry day in October, leaving the

ABOVE LEFT: Green or French beans.

LEFT & ABOVE: Beets.

beets on the surface of the soil to dry. Twist off, rather than cut off, the leaves to avoid bleeding. Place in dry sand in trays, making sure the beets are not touching one another, and store in a cool, frost-free place. In mild areas, where the soil is not susceptible to waterlogging, beets can be left in the ground, provided they are protected from frost.

## BROCCOLI

Broccoli prefers an unshaded, rich, moisture-retentive soil to which lime has been added if the soil is acid, but which has not been freshly manured (best done the previous fall). Never add lime and manure at the same time because they react together and benefit neither. By adding manure in the fall and lime in spring, sufficient time will

have elapsed to prevent problems. Avoid planting in an area where the previous crop belonged to the brassica family (i.e., cabbage, rutabaga/swede, rape, mustard, etc.). Sow seeds outdoors in a seedbed in late April to May, sowing the seeds very thinly in ½-in (1.2-cm) deep drills with about 6in (15cm) of spacing in between.

Thin the seedlings as they grow, increasing spacings between the plants to about 3in (7.5cm). When seedlings are about 3 inches high (June or July), transplant them to their final growing positions. Water the day before lifting,

then plant firmly about an inch deeper than they were when growing in the seedbed, allowing spacings between plants of about 12in (30cm) for green-sprouting varieties, 18in (45cm) for purple and white varieties.

The time from sowing to harvesting is about 12 weeks for the green-sprouting varieties and about 44 weeks for the purple or white varieties, which take longer to mature.

FAR LEFT: Purple-sprouting broccoli.

ABOVE: Broccoli.

## BRUSSELS SPROUTS

Brussels sprouts like an unshaded, rich and moisture-retentive soil to which lime has been added if the soil is acid. Do not add fresh manure, which is best done the previous fall. Avoid planting in an area where the previous crop also belonged to the brassica family. Sow seeds outdoors in a seedbed in early March under cloches or from late March to mid April without. Sow the seeds very thinly in drills ½-in (1.2-cm) deep, allowing about 6in (15cm) between rows.

As the seedlings grow, thin them out to about 3in (7.5cm) apart. Once the plants are 4–6in (10–15cm) high (late May/early June), transplant them

to their final growing positions. Water the seedbed the day before lifting, then plant the seedlings in rows, their lowest leaves just above the soil level, spacing the plants about 2½ft (75cm) apart. The time from sowing to harvesting is between 28 weeks (early varieties) and 36 weeks (late varieties).

## CABBAGES

Spring Cabbage Sow the seeds outdoors in a seedbed, preferably in unshaded, rich and moisture-retentive soil to which lime has been added if the soil is acid. Do not add fresh manure (best done the previous fall). Avoid planting in an area where the previous crop was one of the brassica family. Sowing time is late July to early August. Sow the seeds very thinly in

drills ½-in (1.2-cm) deep with about 6in (15cm) between rows. Thin out seedlings to about 3in (7.5cm) apart.

Once the plants have five or six leaves (late September/early August), transplant them to their final growing positions. Water the seedbed the day before lifting, then plant the seedlings slightly deeper than they were in the seedbed in rows about 6in (15cm) apart, with about 12in (30cm) between rows. Alternatively, the plants may be thinned in March to provide spring greens. The time from sowing to harvest is about 35 weeks.

FAR LEFT: Brussels sprouts.

ABOVE: Spring cabbage.

deep with about 6in (15cm) between rows. As the seedlings grow, thin them out to about 3in (7.5cm) apart.

Once the plants have five or six leaves (May or June), transplant them to their final growing positions. Water the seedbed the day before lifting, then plant the seedlings, slightly deeper than they were when in the seedbed, in rows about 12in (30cm) apart with about 12 inches between rows. The time from sowing to harvesting is 20–35 weeks.

**Winter and Savoy Cabbages** Sow the seeds in seedbeds outdoors, preferably in unshaded, rich and moisture-retentive soil to which lime has been added if the soil is acid. Do not add fresh manure (best done the previous fall). Avoid areas where brassicas were previously grown. Sowing time is from late March to early May. Sow the seeds very thinly in drills ½-in (1.2-cm) deep, with about 6in (15cm) between rows. As the seedlings grow, thin them out to about 3in (7.5cm) apart.

Once the plants have five or six leaves (July), transplant them to their final growing positions. Water the seedbed the day before lifting, then plant the seedlings slightly deeper than they were when in the seedbed, in rows about 12in (30cm) apart with about 12 inches between rows. The time from sowing to harvesting is 20–35 weeks.

**Summer Cabbage** Sow the seeds in a seedbed outdoors, preferably in an unshaded, rich and moisture-retentive soil to which lime has been added if the soil is acid. No not add fresh manure (best done the previous fall). Avoid planting in areas where other brassicas were previously grown. Sowing time is from late March to early May. Sow seeds very thinly in drills ½-in (1.2-cm)

Savoy cabbage.

## CARROTS

Home-grown carrots may not look as perfect as the ones produced for supermarkets, but they have infinitely more flavour. Carrots prefer a light, stone-free soil. Never sow seeds onto freshly manured soil. Sow outdoors in open ground in early March under cloches or without cloches from March to the end of June. Sow the seeds very thinly in ½-in (1.2-cm) deep drills with about 8in (20cm) between rows. As the seedlings grow, thin them out to about 3in (7.5cm) apart. Discard the thinnings, which do not transplant well and which will attract carrot root fly if left on the soil. The time from sowing to harvesting is about 12 weeks for baby carrots and about 16 weeks for main-crop.

To store late-cropping carrots, lift them, cut off the foliage, and bury them in dry sand in trays, making sure the carrots are not touching one another. Store in a dark, cool but frost-free place.

In areas where the soil is not susceptible to waterlogging, the foliage can be removed and the carrots left in the ground, provided they are protected from frost.

## CAULIFLOWER

Avoid freshly manured soil (the excessive nitrogen will make the growth leafy at the expense of producing

florets). Sow outdoors in a seedbed in a slightly acid (pH 6) soil. Sow the seeds very thinly, from late March to early May, in drills ½-in (1.2-cm) deep with about 6in (15cm) between rows. As the seedlings grow, thin them out to about 3in (7.5cm) apart.

Once the plants have five or six leaves (late June/July), transplant them to their final growing positions. Water the seedbed the day before lifting, then plant the seedlings in rows at the same level as they were in the seedbed. Space the plants 2ft (60cm) apart for summer and autumn varieties, and 2½ft (75cm) apart for winter varieties. The time from sowing to harvest is 18–24 weeks for summer and autumn varieties, and 40–50 weeks for winter varieties.

## CELERY

The ideal environment for growing celery is one where there are no weather or temperature extremes. Seeds may be sown outdoors once all risk of a frost occurring has passed. The soil must be well-prepared by digging it over, removing stones and weeds and mixing in a well-rotted manure. A light sprinkling of general-purpose granular fertilizer may be raked in around a week before planting out seedlings.

Plants may be started off by sowing seeds during March and April. Fill a tray or pot with seed compost, levelling it and allowing it to settle. Celery seed is particularly fine and difficult to handle, but should be sown lightly across the surface of the compost (it may be easier to take a pinch of seed at a time). Water by standing the tray or pot in a larger tray of water, allowing the water to soak up into the compost rather than disturbing the seeds by watering from the top. Cover with a thin layer of vermiculite and place the tray or pot in a location where there is constant warmth, a heated propagator on a windowsill or a greenhouse being ideal for the task. Keep the compost moist, never letting it dry out. If a propagator is used, remove the seedlings once they have germinated and formed leaves. Pot them on, using 3-in (7.5-cm) pots filled with multi-purpose compost. Water the plants in. After five weeks, or when the

seedlings have reached 3–4in (8–10cm) in height, the plants can be hardened off in a cold frame or sheltered outdoor location. In May or June, when weather conditions permit, plant them on into their final positions.

Plant out the seedlings in deep trenches, with the crown of each plant at ground level. Leave a space of 10–12in (25–30cm) between plants, and arrange them in a grid rather than a row for best results. Water plants in thoroughly.

Celery is usually harvested from August onwards until the first autumn frosts. Once the celery has reached the required size, harvest it either by cutting off the plant just above the soil line, taking all the stalks together as one head, or harvest the outer stalks leaving the inner ones intact. Wash the stalk bulb or stalks and dry. Stored in the fridge the celery will last for two weeks. It will blanch naturally.

Watering regularly and frequently is the key to producing good celery.

Keep the plants weed-free to avoid competition for nutrients and moisture. Feed once with a liquid fertilizer at around four weeks after planting out to help the celery along.

Although celery will blanch naturally after it is picked, and some varieties are self-blanching, some gardeners blanch the stalks while they are growing in order to reduce bitterness and to produce the desirable pale stems. Soil or mulch built up around the stalks, around four weeks before harvesting, will produce this result.

## CHILIES, CAPSICUMS & EGGPLANTS (AUBERGINES)

Chilies, capsicums and eggplants (aubergines) are usually regarded as crops for warmer climates, but further north they can be grown successfully under glass or in polytunnels. All need a long season to mature, so have the seeds planted in small pots by the end of February or middle of March and into their final growing spots (or pots) by June, by which time they can also be grown outdoors, provided that the winter frosts are well and truly over. All three of these delicious crops are grown in the same way and there are plenty of great varieties from which to choose.

Full sun and a soil rich in organic material will provide the best growing conditions for all three, and patios, roof

Celery (opposite) and eggplants (right).

gardens or balconies are ideal locations where they can catch the sun.

Growing from seed and planting out is identical in each case. To start them off, fill pots (ideally 3in/7–5cm deep) with seed compost, gently firming it down and levelling off the tops. Scatter a thin layer of seeds over the surface; don't sow too many, as most of the seeds will germinate. Sprinkle over a fine layer of vermiculite, then water in.

What you do next depends on the space and resources at your disposal. To encourage germination, a constant temperature of around 70°F (21°C) needs to be maintained, for which a special heat pad, propagator – or for a more makeshift arrangement, a window sill above a radiator – will suffice. The pots can also be covered with polythene bags. Germination will vary between one and three weeks depending on varieties. Once the seedlings appear, start to reduce the temperature gradually, continuing to ensure that the plants do not dry out. Transplant the seedlings into pots of their own when they have grown a second set of leaves. Do this carefully, loosening the compost and gently lifting the seedlings out without touching the roots. The same pots as before can be used, but this time allow only one seedling per pot. Use a multi-purpose compost,

Sweet or bell peppers.

peppers regularly and also mist the plants to maintain a damp atmosphere. If you do not have a warm, sunny and sheltered spot outside, these plants are best kept permanently under glass.

Harvesting is between late June and September: use a knife or scissors to remove the fruit. Capsicums mature from green to red; chilies can be picked and used when green or left to redden and mature. Pick eggplants when they have reached the optimum size for the variety, and when the fruit has assumed its characteristic glossy appearance. An eggplant will produce up to five fruits. When autumn arrives, remove the plants and hang them up to allow the remaining fruit to continue ripening.

If necessary, use sticks or canes to support the plants once they reach 8in (20cm) or so; it is a good idea to pinch out the growing tips to encourage a bushier plant with more fruit. If grown in a container, plants will need to be given a liquid feed throughout the season. A tomato fertilizer is suitable for the purpose, but any liquid feed with a high potash content may be used. Don't use high-nitrogen fertilizers; this will only result in very leafy plants with few fruits.

Chilies, capsicums and eggplants are very thirsty plants, so never allow their compost to dry out; in hot weather, water several times a day, as

levelled and tapped down, and with a dibber make a hole, planting the seedling with its leaves just above the surface. Place the plants in a greenhouse, conservatory or on a sunny window sill. When the roots start to come out of the drainage holes, it is time to move the plants into larger 5-in (12–13-cm) pots.

Plants can go outside once all risk of frost has passed, first hardening them off for a few days by placing them outside only during the day. Capsicums and chilies can be grown on in 1.3-gallon (5-litre) containers, but eggplants do better if they can be got into the ground, either in a greenhouse or polytunnel. Water chilies, eggplants and

Chilies (above left) and cucumbers (opposite).

steady growth without check will produce the best crops.

Eggplants are subject to red spider and whitefly. Dampness will ward off red spider, and whitefly can be sprayed or removed using a vacuum cleaner (if you shake the plant, the flies will take off and you can catch them on the wing). Most varieties of sweet pepper are now disease-resistant.

## CUCUMBERS

Sow seeds indoors in pots of compost or outdoors in open ground. If outdoors, choose a sheltered site in summer (light shade is tolerated) with moisture-retentive, humus-rich soil.

Sow mid-April if starting plants off indoors. Using 2–3-in (5–7.5-cm) pots filled with seed compost, sow two seeds on their edges per pot, at a depth of ½in (1.2cm), removing the weaker seedling at a later stage. Harden off the seedlings, planting them out from late May to early June, with 15–18in (38–45cm) spacings between plants for climbing varieties, and 30in (75cm) for trailing varieties. Plant out seedlings at intervals to provide a succession of cucumbers, while pinching out the growing tips of the plants after six or seven leaves have developed will encourage fruiting on the side shoots.

Sow seeds outdoors from May to early June. Sow two or three seeds together, on their edges, at a depth of 1in (2.5cm) under cloches or glass

jars, allowing 15–18in (38–45cm) between groups if a climbing variety, or 30in (75cm) between groups if a trailing variety. Remove the weaker

seedlings at a later stage. Pinching out the growing tips of the plants after six or seven leaves have developed will encourage fruiting on side shoots.

Once the seeds have germinated and shoots are visible, thin out the seedlings, spacing them about 1½in (3.7cm) apart.

Transplant the seedlings in June or early July when they are about 8in (20cm) long and of a similar thinness to a pencil. Water the bed the day before lifting if the earth is dry. Use a dibber to make holes about 9in (23cm) apart in the main bed, and plant each seedling into a hole.

The time from sowing to harvesting is about 30 weeks for early varieties and about 45 weeks for late varieties.

## LEEKS

Leeks prefer an open site that has been well-dug and preferably manured the previous fall. Alternatively, garden compost or well-rotted manure can be incorporated before planting.

For main-crop leeks, sow seed from late March to April directly into a seedbed about ½-in (1.2-cm) deep in rows about 6in (15cm) apart.

## LETTUCES

Use light, friable, well-drained soil to which lime has been added if the soil is acid, and which has recently had organic matter added. Sow seeds from late March to July in seedbeds or in open ground. Sow the seeds very thinly in ½-in (1.2-cm) deep drills, leaving about 6in (15cm) between rows in seedbeds or 10–12in (25–30cm) between rows in open ground. Successive small sowings will extend the number of lettuces to be

harvested without producing a glut.

As they grow, thin the seedlings in open ground to about 6–12in (15–20cm) apart, depending on the variety; transplant the seedlings from the seedbed when the plants are about 2in (5cm) high, planting them in rows with about 6–12in in between, depending on the variety, and with 10–12in (25–30cm) between rows. The time from sowing to harvesting is 6–14 weeks depending on the variety.

## ONIONS

Using onion sets, rather than seeds, is an easier option where the beginner is concerned, and even experienced growers often prefer growing onions this way. Sets are immature onion bulbs and, as such, have more stored energy within them than seed. They are also more reliable, disease-resistant, and only slightly more expensive to buy than seed.

Plant onion sets in spring, two to four weeks before the last frosts, and use bulbs that are less than $^3/_4$in (19mm) in diameter. Onion sets should be spaced from 4–6in (10–15cm) apart,

depending on the desired size of the mature bulbs. Press bulbs gently into the soil to about an inch (2.5cm) deep, so that their pointed tips just break the surface.

Sets can also be planted in September or October, which enables them to form strong seedlings that will overwinter and get off to a good start in spring. They usually provide a harvestable crop in June, which is a month or two earlier than spring-planted sets.

Many varieties, however, are not available as sets, and seed-grown onions seem to store better when harvested.

You can, however, grow your own sets from seed, saving them to plant out the next season. Seeds can be started indoors and set in the soil as transplants or sown directly outside into the soil. Transplants may also be purchased in bunches from garden centres or seed catalogues, but they are expensive. Direct-seeding is impractical for long-season onions in most home situations, but is suitable for scallions (spring onions).

Onions are frost-tolerant and like cool, wet spring weather. Being light feeders, they prefer rich, well-drained soil with a pH of 6.2–6.8. Onions are best grown in raised beds about 4in (10cm) high and 20in (50cm) wide, with 1–2in (2.5–5cm) of compost worked into the soil. Be sure to water consistently and keep weeds under control while onions are maturing.

Sow onion seeds very thinly in spring or autumn in ½-inch (1.2-cm) deep drills, leaving about 10–12in (25–30cm) between rows. The soil should be open, rich, well-drained, well-dug and lime added if acid. Do not sow onto a freshly manured bed, and avoid planting in an area where the previous crop was also a member of the onion family.

Thin spring-sown onion seedlings in stages to about 2–4in (5–10cm), being sure to remove all thinnings (they may be used as scallions or spring onions) to prevent attack from onion fly. Thin autumn-sown seedlings to about 1in (2.5cm), making sure all thinnings are removed. In spring, further thin the seedlings to about 2–4in (5–10cm) between plants, remembering that closer spacings will give smaller onions than wider ones.

Onions must be thoroughly dried before storage. If the weather is fine, they may be laid on the surface of the soil to dry naturally, otherwise spread them out under cover. Once dry, remove the dead leaves before storing. Onions are ready for harvesting at around 22 weeks from the time of planting.

## PARSNIPS

Parsnips require a long growing season, but they are available as a fresh vegetable throughout the winter, actually improving if frost gets to the roots. Parsnips will thrive in most deep, well-dug soils, to which lime has been added if the soil is acid, and which should preferably have been manured for a previous crop.

To produce long, straight parsnips, the bed needs to be stone-free. Seeds may be sown outdoors in March, into ½-in (1.2-cm) deep drills, with about three seeds every 6in (15cm), and with rows about 12in (30cm) apart. Once seeds have germinated, and the shoots are visible, thin out to one seedling per position, discarding the thinnings. To store late-cropping parsnips, lift the crop, remove the foliage, and store in dry sand in trays, ensuring that the parsnips are not touching one another. Keep in a dark, cool but frost-free place.

In areas where the soil is not susceptible to waterlogging, the foliage may be cut off and the parsnips left in the ground until required, provided they are protected from frost.

## PEAS

Peas sown in cold, wet ground are likely to rot off, so make sure the soil has had time to warm up sufficiently by covering it with polythene before sowing, and by later protecting the seedlings with fleece. Sow shorter varieties in a flat trench, 12in (30cm) deep and 10in (25cm) wide. Sow peas in open ground in light shade. It is essential that the soil is well-drained but moisture-retentive, and has been deeply dug. Preferably it will have been manured the previous fall. Sow seeds under cloches in late February or early

March for a May/June crop, in late March/early April for a June/July crop, and in late June to early July for an autumn crop.

Sow peas in small trenches 6in (15cm) wide, 2in (5cm) deep and spaced to accommodate the expected height of the particular variety being grown; this will typically be 2–3ft (60–90cm) apart for short varieties and 5–6ft (1.5–1.8m) apart for tall varieties

Press the pea seeds into the bottom of the drills in two rows along each side of each drill, with about 3in (7.5cm) between seeds, staggering the pea seeds in the rows. Cover with soil.

Support for the peas, in the form of netting, canes or trellises, depends on the variety being grown. Dwarf varieties (growing up to 18in/45cm high) normally require no support, but for the taller-growing varieties, strong support will be needed. Where necessary, this should be introduced when the seedlings are about 3in (7.5cm) high.

## POTATOES

It is useful to choose the right varieties for your culinary needs before you start. There are around 400 potato varieties available, and some are better than others for boiling, roasting, mashing, salads, etc.

Unlike most vegetables, potatoes prefer soil that is slightly acid, and they should be planted as far away as

possible from places where lime has been applied. They are, however, greedy feeders, so a good amount of manure or compost, worked into the soil, will benefit them greatly as well as improve the texture of the soil.

There is no mystery attached to the process of chitting potatoes. All it means is that when you get your seed potatoes you put them in a cool but frost-free place where they get some light but not direct sunlight; near to a north-facing window in a frost-free

shed would be ideal. The potatoes will then grow short, stubby shoots, which will get them off to a fast start when planted out. With maincrop, some suggest rubbing off all but three shoots to get larger potatoes. Frost is the big enemy so you need to keep an eye on the weather. Usually mid-March is about the right time to plant your earlies, with maincrop planted a few weeks later. If, after planting, the leaves (haulm) begin to show through and frost is threatening, the plants will need protection by bringing earth over from the sides to cover the haulm or by covering with fleece.

To plant, make a hole with a trowel and pop the seed potato in, or a trench may be drawn (take a draw hoe and scrape a trench) and the potatoes placed in it. Then soil is brought over from the sides to cover the potatoes.

Traditional planting distances are as follows:

First Earlies, Second Earlies and Salad varieties: 12in/30cm apart and 4in/10cm deep in rows 18in/45cm apart.

Maincrop varieties: 15in/40cm apart and 4in/10cm deep in rows 24in/60cm apart.
Maincrop types tend to store better but are at more risk of getting blight than the faster types, which are usually harvested before the blight periods begin.

As the plants grow, earth from the sides of the rows needs to be drawn up over the plants in a process known as earthing up. The potato tubers, which are the actual potatoes you will eventually eat, tend to grow towards the surface and they will turn green if light gets to them, making them unfit to eat, which is why earthing up these tubers is so important and will also increase the crop. Remember, also, that covering up some of the leaves will not harm the plant or slow down its growth.

Potatoes are greedy feeders, so extra fertilizer needs to be added after a month or so when the plants are well-established. Use a specifically formulated potato fertilizer or an organic fertilizer such as fish, blood and bone. Good results can also be had from using a liquid comfrey feed which, in this form, makes itself immediately available to the plants.

In dry weather, keep the potatoes well-watered. If the water supply is irregular the yield will be reduced and the potatoes may suffer cracking from uneven growth.

New potatoes will be ready for harvesting at 8–12 weeks from the time of planting. Be aware that the longer potatoes are left in the ground the more they will mature, making them that much more susceptible to blight and other unwelcome pests and diseases.

## RADISHES

Spring and autumn sowings may be made outdoors in open ground, but summer sowings require slight shade. Radishes enjoy a well-drained soil with plenty of humus added. Do not, however, sow on a freshly manured bed.

Summer varieties may be grown under cloches in January or February in mild areas, but cloches are not normally required once March is over. If winter varieties are preferred, sow from July–August.

Sow radish seeds in ½-in (1.2-cm) deep drills at intervals of about 1in (2.5cm), leaving about 6in (15cm) between rows (for winter varieties, leave 9in/22cm between rows). Successive,

small sowings of radish seeds, every two or three weeks, will extend the harvest without producing a glut. The time from sowing to harvesting is 3–6 weeks (summer varieties), 10–12 weeks (winter varieties).

## SPINACH

Spinach is most often credited as being packed with iron, but it is also a rich source of vitamins A and C, thiamin, potassium and folic acid (one of the B-complex vitamins).

Spinach likes a moist but not waterlogged soil containing a good amount of organic matter. It does not like acid soils, and pH should be from 6.3–6.8. Sow seeds outdoors in open

ground in early spring, or stagger the crop by sowing part rows every few weeks. The last sowing should be about 50–60 days before the first frosts. Winter varieties should be grown in open, unshaded, well-drained soil from August–September for harvesting from October–April. Sow seeds very thinly in 1-in (2.5-cm) deep drills about 12in (30cm) apart.

Thin the seedlings as they grow to provide space between plants of about 9in (23cm). Discard the thinnings – they will not transplant. To prolong cropping, pick off any seed heads as they appear. Time from sowing to harvest is from 8–14 weeks.

## RUTABAGA (SWEDES)

Similar to the turnip but much easier to grow, rutabaga has the alternative name of 'swede', which is a contraction of 'swedish turnip'. Rutabaga, surprisingly, is a member of the brassica family, therefore club root, which is a fungal disease, will be a problem if it is already in the soil: it is important, therefore, that it is not grown on sites that have been used for other brassicas for at least two years.

These are slow-growing vegetables, taking 20–26 weeks to reach maturity. They are hardy and best left in the ground over winter until required. Although they are harvested and stored as other root crops, they are at

their best within a week of lifting.

Sow seeds outdoors in open ground, preferably in light, humus-rich soil with no tendency to dryness. Avoid acid soil, having added lime if required, and it should preferably have been manured for a previous crop.

Sow the seeds very thinly in ½–1-in (1.2–2.5-cm) deep drills about 15in (38cm) apart from late May to early June. Thin the seedlings, as they grow, to about 9in (23cm) between plants. Discard the thinnings – they will not transplant.

## SWEET CORN (CORN)

Sweet corn (maize or Indian corn) is deep-rooted and does not grow well in clay-based soils. Planting out in a large block is advisable, in that the plant is wind-pollinated, and this will allow pollen from the male flowers to fall down onto the female tassels from which the cobs will grow. Plant seeds out in April, putting out plug-grown

plants in late May or June, in a location where there is full sun and shelter from strong winds. (Plug plants work well, transplanting easily and establishing quickly.)

To start seeds off indoors, fill 3-in (7.5-cm) pots with compost, making a 1-in (2–3-cm) deep hole in each with a dibber or the end of a pencil. Put two seeds in each hole, cover, and water. Leave the pots on a window sill to germinate. Remove the weaker seedling when growth of about an inch has been achieved. Place the pots outside in a shady location for a week or so to harden off before planting out.

Before planting out, dig out the intended bed deeply, mixing in well-rotted manure; ideally, this should have been done the previous autumn. Closer to the time of planting, remove weeds and large stones, digging over the ground. Level the ground and rake over. Make individual holes for each plant and gently firm them into the soil. Plant in blocks at least 13ft$^2$ (1.2m$^2$), leaving 12–14in (30–35cm) between plants and roughly 2ft (60cm) between rows. Use protective fleece in cold spells when the plants are still vulnerable. Water regularly, especially once cobs begin to form. Take care, when using a Dutch hoe to slice off weeds, not to damage the plant's surface-growing roots. These can be protected by building up soil around the stems in mounds, which will also encourage further stabilizing roots to form, allowing the plants to cope better in stronger winds.

It is possible to undercrop between plants where space is limited. Sweet

corn's relatively compact foliage will allow sufficient light to penetrate and smaller vegetables grown in between, such as dwarf beans, radishes or lettuce, will not be crowded out.

Each individual plant will produce one or two cobs. Watch the tassels at the ends of the cobs: the time for harvesting will have arrived when these turn brown. Double-test for ripeness by removing part of a husk and squeezing a kernel inside. If the juice from the kernel appears milky, then the cob is ready. To harvest a cob, twist it away from the plant. It is possible to freeze cobs for longer-term storage.

## SWEET POTATOES

Sweet potatoes are native to Central and South America where the climate is warm for most of the time, and they are cultivated commercially in most southern states of the USA. It is possible, however, to grow some varieties in more northerly climes, as long as the temperature remains at 60°F (15°C) towards the end of the growing season. These tender vegetables are related to morning glory (genus *Ipomoea*). They grow on vines that cover the soil, setting roots as they go. There are also bush varieties, and these have short vines and work better in areas where there is limited space.

Don't expect to grow sweet potatoes from seed. It is necessary to obtain 'slips' from an established vine from a local nursery. A common science project for schoolchildren entails placing a sprouting sweet potato, suspended on toothpicks, in a glass of water. The vine grows out the top and the roots grow down into the water. The vines growing from the top are usually white before gradually turning green with leaves. It is therefore possible to grow your own slips from a sweet potato, but it is still easier to buy them, which will ensure that the plants are as disease-resistant as possible.

Plant the slips directly into the soil in early summer when the ground temperature reaches 70°F (21°C). First make a wide, raised ridge in the ground

about 8in (20cm) high. Plant the slips 12–15in (30–38cm) apart in the highest part of the ridge. As mentioned before, sweet potatoes love the heat so it would be beneficial to use black plastic covering to keep the soil warm. Allow about 3–4ft (1m or so) between rows as the vines need plenty of space.

You won't have to worry about weeds, since the vines will choke out anything that grows in their way. Water regularly and fertilize with a 5-10-10 water-soluble fertilizer every three weeks once they have become established. Most sweet potatoes take 100–110 days from slip to harvestable vegetable. Water only sporadically during the last three to four weeks before harvest.

## TOMATOES

Seeds may be started off indoors by sowing them in pots of compost, although an alternative is to purchase young tomato plants in late May/early June. Tomatoes are grown mostly in greenhouses, where the climate is uncertain, although a few varieties can be grown outdoors.

Tomatoes like a nice warm spot in full sun, and at least eight hours of sunlight a day, or they become spindly and produce little mature fruit. They must be sheltered from the wind, or they can be grown against a wall or fence. Keep well away from the potato crop. A well-drained, fertile soil is an essential growing medium, preferably

one that has been manured for a previous crop, otherwise apply a general fertilizer about two weeks before planting. Never apply fresh manure just before planting.

Sow seeds from mid March to early April in shallow drills in seed trays. When seedlings reach the three-leaf stage, prick out, transferring them to larger containers and allowing 2–3in (5–7.5cm) between plants. Alternatively, plant the seedlings individually in 2–3-in diameter peat pots.

Another method is to sow two or three seeds directly into 2–3-in diameter peat pots or peat blocks, thinning out the seedlings when they are at the three-leaf stage.

When the plants are about 7–8in (17–20cm) high, whatever the sowing method used, and once all danger of frost has passed (late May/early June), harden off the plants and transplant them outdoors (purchased tomato plants can also be planted out at this time).

The plants should be set about 18in (45cm) apart, with a 4-ft (120-cm) plus stake provided for each plant if they are tall-growing or cordon varieties. As the plants grow, tie in the stems to the stake at 8-in (20-cm) intervals. When the first fruits begin to form, the plant will produce side shoots in between the main stem and the leaf stems. If allowed to remain, they will grow and produce a mass of foliage but few tomatoes. Therefore, they should be removed by pinching them out with the fingers. Once each plant has developed four or five trusses, pinch out the growing tip to stop further vertical growth.

It is important to water tomatoes regularly but without letting the compost become waterlogged. Irregular watering often results in split fruit. The time from sowing to harvesting is about 20 weeks.

**TURNIPS**

Grow turnips outdoors in open ground, preferably in light, humus-rich soil, avoiding potential dry areas. Also avoid acid soil, adding lime if required. The soil should preferably have been manured for a previous crop.

For an early crop, start sowing seeds in March in ½-in (1.2-cm) deep drills, with about 9in (22cm) between rows. Sow thinly and cover with soil. Making repeated small sowings every month until early July will ensure a longer season of fresh turnips than a single sowing. Thin out the seedlings so that they are about 5in (13cm) apart.

For the main storage crop, plant turnips in late June or early July, so that roots can develop in the warmer weather, late plantings being less susceptible to damage by turnip-root maggot.

## VEGETABLE MARROWS, ZUCCHINI (COURGETTES) & SQUASHES

This method can also be used to produce zucchini (courgettes) and the various squashes.

In late April, sow seeds indoors in pots filled with seed compost. Sow two seeds on their edges in a 2–3-in (5–7.5-cm) pot, at a depth of ½in (1.2cm), removing the weaker seedling in due course. Harden off and plant out the seedlings from late May to early June,

OPPOSITE: Turnips.

ABOVE RIGHT: Vegetable marrow.

RIGHT: Yellow zucchini (courgettes).

allowing 15–24in (38–60cm) between plants for bush varieties, 18in (45cm) for climbing varieties, and 4ft (120cm) for trailing varieties. Pinch out the growing tips of trailing varieties when they reach 24in (60cm) long.

Alternatively, sow seed outdoors from late May to early June in a very sheltered site (light shade is tolerated) with a moisture-retentive, humus-rich soil. Sow two or three seeds on their edges at a depth of 1in (2.5cm), under cloches or glass jars, allowing 15–24in (38–60cm) between plants for bush varieties, 18in (45cm) for climbing varieties and 4ft (120cm) for trailing

varieties. Remove the weaker seedlings in due course. Pinch out the growing tips of trailing varieties when they reach 24in (60cm) long.

Failure of the fruits to form is common, especially in dull, damp summers, while planting in soil that is too rich may result in luxuriant foliage but few fruits.

LEFT: Pumpkins.

ABOVE: Carnival squashes.

OPPOSITE ABOVE: Rosemary, parsley and sage.

OPPOSITE BELOW: Basil is excellent with tomato-based dishes.

in flavour. In fact, herbs grow best when soils contain only adequate organic matter. In areas where winter temperatures never drop very far below freezing, there is the opportunity to grow many of the shrubby Mediterranean aromatics, and rosemary, lavender, marjoram and santolina, for example, will grow larger and more attractive with each passing year.

In fact, many herbs originated in Mediterranean lands and so appreciate free-draining soils. Drainage can be improved by adding grit to planting holes. Avoid overfeeding; simply place a dressing of manure or compost around the bases of the plants each fall, and only add liquid fertilizer during the growing season if plants appear to be struggling.

## GROWING HERBS

Herbs are defined as any of the herbaceous plants valued for their flavour, fragrance or medicinal properties. Herbs are easy to grow, and impart a finer, fresher, more vibrant flavour to food than the dried alternatives, which quickly go stale if kept in the cupboard for too long. Be sure to choose the right herb for the right location; most enjoy a sunny spot, and only a few, such as angelica, sweet woodruff and sweet cicely, are better grown in partial shade. Most do not require a highly fertile soil, which tends to produce excessive foliage that is poor

Most herbs are tough, wild plants which will thrive when given the luxurious conditions of a garden. When planting culinary herbs, divide them into those that enjoy full sun, such as rosemary, thyme, sweet basil, French tarragon, sage and oregano, and those happier in partial shade, such as sorrel, mizuna, rocket, mustard, parsley and chervil.

Like all plants, herbs fall into two categories: annual and perennial. Annuals live for a single year, flowering and developing seeds from which the next generation will grow. Perennial plants last for many years, and deserve to be given a permanent position where they can flower every year.

Annual herbs include basil, cilantro (coriander) and marjoram, while the perennials include mint (whose roots must be contained to avoid it running amok, but which can be grown in pots sunk into the soil), thyme, rosemary, lavender and sage. Chives, garlic, and the other members of the onion family, are perennial plants originally grown from seed but

LEFT: Chives, the smallest member of the onion family, have a milder, subtler taste.

OPPOSITE ABOVE: Dill in flower. It is excellent with fish.

OPPOSITE BELOW: Thyme is good in chicken dishes.

the back door, so that they are within easy reach of the kitchen, and where they can scent the air on a hot summer's day.

The most common of the traditional culinary herbs are:
Basil
Chives
Cilantro (coriander)
Dill
Marjoram
Mint
Oregano
Parsley
Rosemary
Sage
Summer savory
Thyme
Winter savory

more often from bulbs. Some herbs fall into the biennial category, which means they flower and develop seeds in their second season, and include parsley and caraway.

Herbs may be grown among vegetables, in formal parterres or with flowers in beds or herbaceous borders. They can even be grown in pots on the patio, or in hanging baskets near to

Most herbs can be grown from seed and sown directly into the soil. For an early harvest, start the seeds off in shallow trays indoors in late winter, then transplant the seedlings out after all risk of frost has passed. Harvest the leaves when the plant has sufficient foliage. Don't pick too many at a time, as this will weaken the plant.

The flavour of the leaves are at their best just before the plant comes into flower. Most herbs also produce seeds that can be used for flavouring food, and these can be gathered and stored once flowering is over and seed heads have formed.

# GROWING FRUIT

## Soft Fruits

Seasonal soft fruits, such as strawberries and raspberries, are the true taste of summer, and to grow them in your own backyard, picking them straight from the plant as they ripen, is a real treat. Home-grown fruit does not come any fresher: flavour is more pronounced, hinting of the health benefits in store, and you save money at the same time.

Fruit trees, bushes and plants can be grown anywhere: in flower borders, in vegetable plots, even in containers on patios. Most fruit plants like a sunny, sheltered position in soil that remains moist without becoming waterlogged, and which is not too alkaline (slightly acid to neutral soil of pH 6–7 is ideal).

If soil is sandy, or there is heavy clay, dig in plenty of well-rotted organic matter before planting, such as garden compost or blended farmyard manure. This improves the ability of thin soil to hold water and adds nutrients at the same time. It also opens up heavy soil so that roots can spread out and grow.

Fruit plants are extremely hardy and are able to tolerate a surprising amount of damage. Birds are not the only pests competing for the first crops,

Home-grown soft fruits are packed full of flavour and goodness.

so protect them with netting, but be sure to keep it taut to stop birds getting caught up in it. Choosing disease-resistant varieties will ensure a good crop.

The best time to buy and transplant is when plants are not growing. Do this in late autumn or early spring when the soil has some residual warmth: in most areas, from mid October–mid December and from late February–early April are the best times.

Be sure to get plants back into the ground within a few days, keeping roots moist at all times. Bushes can stay in their pots until you are ready to plant them, provided they are kept well-watered.

## BLUEBERRIES

Where blueberries are concerned, the first thing to consider are the type you wish to plant. Be sure to pick the variety that fits your available space and climate zone, and always purchase bushes from a reputable supplier.

Like most fruits and vegetables, blueberries require several hours a day in full sun, and anything less will have an impact on yields. Blueberries grow best in a fairly acid soil or one with a pH of 4–4.5. You may need to add sulphur to get the pH into the desired range or alternatively grow the plants in pots containing ericaceous compost, occasionally giving them a high potash feed during the growing season.

The soil should be a loamy mix, with about 4–7 per cent organic matter. Blueberries have shallow roots, making drainage all-important. If soil is clay or poorly drained, then raised beds are a sensible option, or soil can alternatively be built up around the plants. It is always a good idea to introduce compost into your soil preparation.

Blueberries, in general, are self-pollinating, but like most fruits the yield and quality of the fruit can be increased by adding a pollinator bush. As for the number of bushes to plant, four or five are usually enough for an average family, and can easily be handled even in a raised garden bed. The spacing of plants will vary according to variety, but is usually 5 or 6ft (1.5 or 1.8m) for larger varieties. Low bush varieties will typically be spaced about 3ft (1m) apart.

Be sure to plant after all danger of frost has passed. Assuming the soil has already been prepared to suit, dig a hole slightly larger by a few inches than the root ball, placing the plant in the hole, then packing the soil firmly around it. To encourage runner development, cover a little of the bush stems with soil. Given only a modicum of care, blueberries have the potential to last for many years.

## CURRANTS

Red-, black- and whitecurrants are full of antioxidants, vitamin C and minerals. The bushes or canes are very easy to look after, and they can tolerate degrees of sun and shade. The most commonly grown is the blackcurrant.

Plant out bare-rooted stock from October through to March. If a currant bush has already been established in a container, it can be planted out at any time of year, avoiding periods of continual frost or waterlogged soil conditions. Currants are quite accommodating and do well either in sun or in dappled shade, while good air circulation will reduce the risk of fungal diseases. The soil must be well-drained though moist; always avoid dry

planting areas. Dig in plenty of well-rotted manure.

Bare-rooted stock usually comes via mail order as plain stems and roots. On arrival, and before planting out, place roots in a bucket of water and leave for 12–24 hours. Dig a hole that fits the roots comfortably, without bending or breaking them. Place the roots in the hole and replace the soil. Ensure that the base of the stem is level with the soil surface after the soil has been firmed down. Water thoroughly. In the case of an established plant, dig a hole wide enough for the roots and to a depth allowing the soil mark on the stem to match the soil surface. Position the plant and fill in with soil. Water in thoroughly and scatter well-rotted

manure around the plant. Leave a space of 5ft (1.5m) between bushes.

Prune white- and redcurrants to reveal an open centre to the bush, allowing light to come in and air to circulate; this also makes for more convenient picking. When the plant is established, cut away branches that are close to the soil, leaving 4in (10cm) of stem. Prune away other branches to an outward-facing bud, cutting back roughly two-thirds of their length. Allow the bush to grow into the required shape and space in subsequent years, cutting back leading shoots by 50 per cent to an upright bud.

Blackcurrants should be pruned differently: once established, prune down to stubby shoots or leave two

## GOOSEBERRIES

Soil must be fertile, well-drained but moist in order for gooseberries to thrive. Plant out in the autumn, choosing a sunny, sheltered location, in the absence of which, shady, relatively cool conditions will be tolerated. Prepare the ground by forking it over and removing weeds and stones. Dig a planting hole suitable for the root growth, then fork in some well-rotted manure or compost, combined with granules or pellets of general-purpose fertilizer, in the base. Gooseberries are also suitable for container planting.

The size of the planting hole should be around three times the diameter of the roots but no deeper than the roots. Spread out the roots of bare-rooted gooseberries in the prepared planting hole, covering them with soil. Avoid air pockets by placing soil between and around the roots. Firm the soil down and water in. Gooseberry bushes should be spaced at just over 3ft (1m) apart, allowing access for picking; cordons can be spaced at between 14 and 18in (35 and 45cm). Keep well-watered until the plants are established; use a mulch of bark or compost around the plants.

To plant a gooseberry bush in a container, fill the base with a layer of stones to allow for drainage. A terracotta pot around 14in (35cm) deep is ideal. Cover the stones with compost, then lower the roots of the bush down

buds above ground level on each branch. When the first growing season is over, prune down to one strong shoot at soil level. In subsequent years, prune blackcurrants in winter to the shape and size required, leaving the centre open to light and air, and cutting away any older two-year-old branches – identifiable by their grey colour – also any blackened stems. Blackcurrants produce fruit on older growth.

Keep bushes free from surrounding weeds, and remove the suckers of red- or whitecurrants as they appear. Keep plants moist during dry spells, but be aware that overwatering may cause the skins of the fruit to split. Each spring, scatter a new layer of manure around the plants.

Protect the plants with netting or fruit cages, as birds will eat both the fruit and the developing buds. Harvest when the fruit is still firm but ripe. Remove the currants as bunches or strings, or pick individual currants if they are to be eaten straight away. Most soft fruit freezes well.

Currants are extremely versatile used fresh, cooked in pies and tarts, in juices, jellies and jams, and in the exquisite blackcurrant crème de cassis liqueur.

so that the soil mark on the stem matches the rim of the pot. Water in, then firm down the soil. Use a liquid fertilizer once a week.

The first harvest should be ready in late May to early June: remove around half the crop, leaving room for the remaining fruit to grow large. This early crop can be used for cooking. A few weeks after the initial harvest, further crops can be picked.

Net gooseberries when they are fruiting to prevent them from becoming food for the birds. Weight the netting at the edges to stop birds from getting underneath.

Pruned and trained gooseberries will produce the best crops. The aim of winter pruning should be to form a balanced branch structure, while at the same time keeping the centre of the bush open. Cut back leading shoots by a third, then prune back shoots pointing towards the centre of the bush. In summer, side shoots can be pruned back to five leaves to encourage fruiting spurs to develop.

Train single-stemmed cordons against walls or onto canes, tying the leading-shoot tip into the support. As with bushes, prune side shoots back to five leaves during the summer. When winter comes, shorten the main tip by a quarter, and shorten side shoots to three buds, encouraging the formation of new fruit spurs for the following year.

## RASPBERRIES

It is an easy matter to establish and maintain a raspberry patch, and if a mix of different varieties are used, including some of the thornless types, a fruiting season from June right through to the first frosts of autumn can be achieved. It is easiest to buy raspberry canes from a supplier, such as a nursery or garden centre.

Plant out the bare-rooted canes in autumn. Choose a spot in full sun or part shade where there is well-drained soil, having prepared the site several weeks earlier by digging the ground over and incorporating well-rotted

organic matter into the soil. Remove weeds and stones.

Dig a planting hole deep enough for the soil mark on the stems of the canes to remain at the same level as the ground when planted. Carefully spread out the roots, lower the plant into the hole, then fill in with soil, firming it in to prevent air pockets. Water well. Allow around 14–18in (35–45cm) between canes.

Raspberry canes tend to lean sideways, resulting in damaged fruit if left unsupported. Use wire between fence posts or tree stakes placed 10ft (3m) apart, or in a small patch use

single supports with the raspberries trained around them. The supports should be roughly 8ft (2.5m) in height. Prune canes above a bud when they are around 12in (30cm) tall.

Raspberries need plenty of water: keep plants damp throughout the summer, scattering fertilizer over the soil around the canes in spring. It is also a good idea to lay down mulch to help retain moisture levels.

The fruits will redden quickly. Pick them regularly when firm, pulling each raspberry away from its plug, which should be left intact as part of the plant. Once picked, refrigerate the fruit to prevent it from perishing. It should remain fresh for three to six days.

During the autumn, prune fruiting canes back to ground level. Using garden twine, tie in a group of the newly-grown canes, choosing around seven or eight of the strongest which will fruit next year. Remove the older canes. During the winter, cut away ungainly top growth. For later, autumn-fruiting varieties, prune old canes and tie in the new in mid-winter. Old canes that are unlikely to fruit again are recognizable by the peeling, greyish bark on stem and branch.

Canes which show signs of disease or infestation should be removed. It is also good practice to remove those that now block access to your rows of canes or are outside the patch itself. These will block light and air circulation necessary for growth if they are not removed.

## RHUBARB

Contrary to popular belief, rhubarb is actually a vegetable; however, it is treated as though it were a soft fruit for culinary purposes. Cultivated for its delicious, pink stems, rhubarb is a very hardy, frost-resistant plant; in fact, it requires a period of frost in winter in order to produce the best stems. It is important to remember, however, that the leaves contain oxalic acid and are poisonous if consumed. It is only the stems that will be used.

Plant out crowns in late autumn to early winter, October being ideal for the purpose. Rhubarb can be grown in shady areas (potential frost pockets should be avoided) and ideally in positions of partial shade. Rhubarb thrives in slightly acid soils with a pH of between 6 and 6.8. Ground that is prone to waterlogging should be avoided at all costs, and will result in rotting crowns.

Rhubarb will develop an extensive root system, therefore it is worth the effort to dig over the soil four weeks before planting. Remove stones and mix in compost and organic matter. Space rhubarb crowns 3ft (1m) apart in rows 3ft apart. Plant the roots with the crown bud 2in (5cm) below the surface of the soil. The hole for the crown must be dug extra large and composted manure should be mixed with the soil to be placed around the roots. Firm in the soil, keeping it loose over the buds. Water well.

Remove flowers when they appear in early spring, as blooming and seeding will slow down the growth of the stems, with energy being diverted into growing seeds. Fertilizing in the early spring will also increase the rhubarb harvest significantly.

Once the leaves have died back, put down compost around the plants. There are few diseases to watch out for during the year, and as long as the soil is well-drained, the crowns should not succumb to rot. You will notice, if they do, that a fungus at the base of the stems is causing them to turn brown and soft. Remove the plant and destroy it at once.

Established rhubarb plants need to be divided or split into three or four separate crowns roughly every five years. This should be done during winter dormancy, using a spade. When doing this, ensure that each new crown has a bud that will shoot during the coming growing season.

## STRAWBERRIES

Three types of strawberries are commonly grown: June-bearing, Everbearing and Day Neutral, the most popular being the June-bearing. Strawberries grow very well in containers, which is useful if space is at a premium, and they are ideal for growing in raised beds.

Strawberries thrive in well-drained soil in full sun or part shade. It is easiest to grow strawberries from plants bought from a nursery or garden centre. The best time to plant them is in early autumn or spring. If planting in spring, remove any flower buds so that the plant's energy is concentrated on developing roots and becoming established. Space the plants 16in (40cm) apart in rows 3ft (1m) apart. Water well. It is a good idea to mulch the plants with a thick layer of well-rotted manure, compost or straw (some gardeners grow their plants through black polythene). This impenetrable layer will prevent weeds from growing and competing with the plants. It will also keep the soil moist, cutting down on watering.

Flowering starts from early summer onwards, and the fruit will develop from the flowers as they die down. The young fruits now need to be protected from mud damage, and it is an easy matter to mulch with straw or tuck handfuls of straw under the fruit trusses to ensure they are not in direct contact with the soil. Once the fruits have ripened (when they are deep red in colour and slightly soft to the touch), simply pick them gently off the plant.

After the final fruits have been harvested, cut the remaining foliage down to about 4in (10cm) above the crown to allow new leaves to grow. Clear away and burn any debris from around the plants (including removed foliage). This prevents disease from building up around the plants and hampering growth the following year.

Water the plants thoroughly and apply a mulch of well-rotted manure or garden compost to add nutrients to the soil. You will notice, at the end of the fruiting season, that the plants will have developed several runners with small plants growing from them. These grow roots and can become new plants. In late summer, simply insert the individual plantlets attached to the runners into small pots filled with cutting compost. Sever each young plant from its parent once it has rooted.

## GROWING AND MAINTAINING FRUIT TREES

One or two fruit trees should be enough to produce abundant fruit for most needs, given that there is sufficient space in your backyard, while showers of pink or white blossom will gladden the eye in spring. Fruit trees come in all shapes and sizes and so do their roots, which means you can choose exactly the right type for your plot – whether it be a giant tree or one that can be grown in a pot.

### APPLES

Apple trees are likely to yield fruit for over 40 years, and a productive tree will provide a store of apples to last right through until spring. They are usually bought as bare-rooted stock, or you could try growing them from seed if time is on your side. Many believe apples need plenty of room, but they can be accommodated in whatever space is available, be they full-sized trees, bushes, cordons, espaliers trained along walls and fences, or those grown in containers as patio plants. Many apple cultivars are currently available. When making a selection, consider fruit size, taste, colour, blossom period, ripening season, disease-resistance and pollen compatibility, all of which are important factors.

Apple trees are ideally planted between October and December. A position in full sun is desirable, although some shade can be tolerated. The soil should be relatively free-draining, and areas that tend to become waterlogged or which are subject to frost, likely to kill off the blossom, should be avoided at all cost. The type of soil is not crucial, and a medium soil that is slightly acid with moderate fertility would suffice, though extremes of acidity and alkalinity are best avoided.

In general, the advice is to plant two trees to ensure pollination, but in a reasonably populated area a single apple tree is likely to be pollinated by neighbouring trees as bees move from one to another over a wide area. It is probably best to start off with a young tree from a nursery, which will produce apples that much sooner. To plant a bare-rooted tree, prepare the soil around one month ahead. Dig a hole 20–24in (50–60cm) deep and 3ft (1m) wide, then mix in plenty of well-rotted organic material. Remember that the soil needs to be at a medium level of fertility, otherwise the tree will take on too much growth but produce very little fruit. If the planting location is in the centre of a lawn, also mix into the planting hole a long-lasting fertilizer such as bonemeal. Position the tree in the hole and fill in with soil, ensuring that the noticeable 'grafting joint', between the rootstock and the scion (the trunk above the joint), is above the level of the soil by 2in (5cm) or more. Use your feet to firm down the soil and water in thoroughly. Some varieties will need support, in which case stakes should be placed 3–4in (8–10cm) away and the tree tied to them. Use plastic rather than metal ties, which will not damage the tree. Check them as the tree grows and readjust as necessary to avoid ties cutting into the trunk.

To train a tree to grow along a fence or wall, choose a south-facing location and ensure that the supporting structure will not collapse under the weight of fruit. A framework of trellis or horizontal wires will permit the branches to be trained into position, while also allowing the tree itself to support much of its own weight. The spacing of wires in the framework should match the distance between the branches or 'arms' of the tree, i.e., around 14–25in (35–50cm) apart. Plant out as above, digging the planting hole out from the side of the wall or fence.

Apples which twist off easily from the tree are likely to be ripe, or you could try one and see. Different varieties fruit at different times, but the season can be prolonged by planting out a selection of varieties which will provide a staggered crop. Take care not to damage or knock apples when harvesting them as they bruise relatively easily, and bruises encourage rot. The sunnier the position of the tree, the more time will be available for

season; summer pruning causes growth to slow down; spring pruning produces a combined effect.

In the case of a one-year-old bare-rooted tree, cut off the top half of the trunk with a pair of secateurs soon after planting. A two-, three- or four-year-old tree should have its black side shoots pruned by one-third between December and February; pink growth from the previous year should be left untouched and only cut away if it has become diseased. Prune above an outward-facing bud. Five-year-old trees are by now mature, having established their shape; prune them to keep the centre clear, removing growth that is weak or diseased. Try to maintain an equal balance between growth produced in the last year, on which apples will grow, and older growth. Cordons need to be pruned in August, with side shoots pruned back to three leaves. Tie down new growth to keep a trained tree growing sideways.

To deter overwintering pests, use a horticultural, oil-based winter wash in December or January. A lighter summer oil may be used during the growing season, and a grease band placed at 20in (50cm) above soil level will protect the tree from moths, the caterpillars of which eat leaves and fruit. Thin out fruit before harvest time; removing small or misshapen apples will give the good apples more of a chance to fill out.

the fruit to ripen. Fruit that ripens later in the season will tend to be more suitable for winter storage. Keep apples in a cool, dark, well-ventilated store such as a dry shed or garage.

Pruning the trees is vital. Pruning at different times of the year produces different effects. Winter pruning during the tree's period of dormancy triggers greater growth in the forthcoming

## CHERRIES

Plant trees at any time between late autumn and early winter when they are dormant, avoiding periods of frost. Choose a site with well-drained, fairly light soil. Soil pH should be between 6 and 7. You can check how well a particular site is draining by digging a planting hole; if rainwater remains in the hole over several days, then waterlogging is a problem. Frost pockets should also be avoided. Cherry trees are not as frequently grown as apples, therefore a pair of trees will be required if your chosen variety is not self-fertilizing.

Dig over the site a few weeks in advance of planting, removing weeds and stones. Before planting the trees, soak the roots. Then use a spade to dig a hole which needs to be at least a third wider than the roots, though no deeper; fork over the soil at the bottom of the hole. Place a stake next to the root before filling in the hole with soil, mounding it towards the base of the tree. Firm the soil down gently with your feet and water in thoroughly. Keep the tree watered until it is well-established, feeding regularly.

Alternatively, half-fill a container or pot with soil-based potting compost, plant the tree, and fill up with more compost. If planting to grow against a wall, plant the tree around 6–8in (15–20cm) away from it. A sunny location is usually required, but there are some dwarf varieties that can be grown on north-facing walls.

Harvest cherries between early June and the end of July, depending on the weather. Pick the cherries with their stalks intact. If, in the run-up to the harvest, the days are rather grey, use a silver-lined reflective material, available from specialist nurseries and garden centres. This is laid on the ground so that light is reflected back up onto the fruit, but laying down pebbles or flints around the base of the tree can achieve much the same purpose.

Pruning is essential. Bushes and trees may be pruned from year two onwards to produce a conical shape with branches shortening towards the top. In April, once the tree is in leaf, cut growth back to a bud or side shoot, cutting the bush back into its ideal conical shape in August. This shape allows light to reach all parts of the tree, and most crucially to the trunk from which new branches will grow. Branches which have borne a crop of fruit for five to six years will begin to weaken, and will need to be cut away. Don't prune cherry trees in winter. Be aware that fruit buds grow on branches which are two or more years old.

To encourage or trigger the growth of a new branch, use a pruning saw to gently score or 'notch' the trunk above a growing node. Sap will then build up at this point and a bud will grow. Make the score horizontally into the bark across the trunk.

Use netting to keep birds away. Netting a dwarf cherry tree is relatively easy but a full-sized tree can be rather more difficult. It is possible to net individual clusters, or use whatever bird-scaring method that is most effective. To deter aphids, plant wild flowers around trees to encourage aphid-eating ladybugs (ladybirds) and lacewings to visit.

## PEACHES & NECTARINES

Peaches have been grown in Asia for more than 2,000 years, produced for centuries in the United States, and thrive on a commercial basis in Mediterranean areas. Peaches are regarded as the 'queen' of fruits, coming second only to apples in popularity because of their food value and fine flavour. Nectarines can be used in the same way as peaches: genetically, the only difference between the two is the absence of fuzz on the nectarine's skin. Usually, nectarines are smaller than peaches, with both red and yellow colouring in the skin and a rather more pronounced aroma.

Both require sunny sites and protection from frost when in blossom. For these reasons they are unsuitable for areas prone to hard frosts. Therefore, the growing of free-standing trees in cooler areas, such as the UK and parts of North America, is not recommended. In cooler climes, however, when grown as fan-trained trees against south-facing walls, large crops of delicious fruit will be produced.

Correct positioning and soil type are the keys to growing peaches and nectarines successfully. Both produce blossom in early spring which, if damaged by frost, will never go on to produce fruit. For this reason a south-facing wall (house walls are ideal), protected from wind, is the only satisfactory site. A fully-grown fan peach tree will have a spread of approximately 16ft (5m) and a height of 8ft (2.5m), so walls need to be large enough to accommodate this growth. Also bear in mind that wire supports will need to be nailed to the wall so that branches can be trained along their length.

Soil must be pre-dug (August is the ideal time) to a depth of 2ft 6in (75cm) a couple of months before planting to allow it to settle. Plenty of compost should be added to make the soil capable of holding water, but at the same time allow the excess to drain away. The soil should be neither too acid nor too alkaline.

Dig a planting hole 6ft (1.8m) by 3ft (1m) to a depth of 2ft 6in (75cm), adding garden compost and/or other organic matter. Scatter two or three handfuls of bonemeal or other long-lasting fertilizer into the hole and dig it in well. Plant the tree, then attach it to the pre-prepared wire frame, training the branches of the tree along the wires as it grows.

## PEARS

Pear trees are widely cultivated across the world, the fruit being juicier than apples and generally softer in texture. The pear belongs in the same plant family as the apple, and bears similar flowers. Being deep-rooted trees, pears prefer a light loamy soil avoiding extremes of pH. The planting site must be sheltered from strong winds, avoiding locations where frost pockets occur. It is more difficult to establish a pear tree in a given location if the soil is allowed to dry out.

Factors to consider are the size of the tree (usually between 10 and 20ft/ 3 and 6m high), the variety and taste of the fruit, and ease of pollination. Varieties such as Conference are self-fertile, otherwise a pair of trees must be planted to ensure fertilization. A single tree in a neighbourhood where there are many backyards is quite likely to be pollinated by adjacent trees, but this cannot always be guaranteed.

Plant bare-rooted trees between December and early March, when they are in their period of dormancy, but ready-grown, potted trees can be planted out at any time of the year. To plant a bare-rooted tree, prepare the soil a month ahead. Dig a hole a little wider and deeper than the roots of the young tree. Mix in plenty of well-rotted organic material, bearing in mind that the soil needs to be at a medium level of fertility. If the chosen

location is in the middle of a lawn, mix in a long-lasting fertilizer such as bonemeal. Place the tree in position and fill in with soil, ensuring that the noticeable grafting joint, between the rootstock and the scion (the trunk above the joint) stands proud of the soil level by 2in (5cm) or more. Firm down the soil with your feet and water in thoroughly. Some varieties will need staking out, in which case use the same method as described in the section on Apples.

If the intention is to train a tree to grow along a supporting fence or wall, choose a south-facing location and ensure that the supporting structure is strong enough to bear the weight of fruit. A framework of horizontal wires will allow the tree to be trained into position while also allowing it to support much of its own weight. The spacing of the wires in the framework should match the distance between the branches or 'arms' of the tree, being around 14–20in (35–50cm) apart. Plant out as above, digging the planting hole out from the side of the wall or fence.

Pear trees tend to drop fruit in early to mid June; don't be alarmed, this is a natural occurrence. A month later, thin the fruit out further to allow the remaining pears to reach a good size. As a rough guide, pears can be thinned to leave around 3–5in (8–12cm) between fruit on the tree.

Depending on the rootstock, a pear tree will produce fruit after 3–5 years and a productive lifespan of up to 200 years may be expected according to variety.

Prune during winter when the trees are dormant, opening a space in the centre to allow light in and air to circulate. The shape of a tree is formed by pruning over the first eight years, allowing eight main fruiting branches to develop. Be gentle, as branches are relatively fragile compared with those of apple trees. Keep an equal balance between older growth and last season's growth. Cordons need to be pruned in August, with side shoots pruned back to three leaves. Tie down new growth to keep a trained tree growing sideways. Pests can be deterred in the same way as for apples (see Apples section above). Expose and kill pear midges when they are still on the ground by raking over the soil surface from late January through to late March, which is also the time when mulch can be spread around trees so that water is retained in the soil. If using compost as a mulch, leave a free space around the trunk.

Pears for storage should be harvested when still firm. They damage easily, so check them thoroughly for bruises. They don't benefit from being wrapped, so arrange them in a single layer on slatted shelves or in storage trays. Store for a few weeks only, after

which they will need to finish off the ripening process. A week before you are ready to eat them, move the pears into a warm spot to ripen up, and eat within a few days.

## PLUMS

October or November are the optimum months for planting out plum trees, but this is also possible, though more risky, from late autumn through to early spring. Plums require warmth and plenty of light, so a moist spot in full sun would be ideal. Avoid frost pockets, and you would be well-advised to choose a late-flowering variety in cooler areas. A good draining soil is important, and remember to plant a pair of trees rather than one if it is not self-pollinating.

If space is at a premium, choose a half-size or small variety which can be trained against a wall. First soak the roots, then use a spade to dig a hole. This needs to be at least a third wider than the roots, though no deeper; fork over the soil at the bottom of the hole. Stake the tree out, placing the stake next to the root before filling in the hole with soil, mounding it towards the base of the tree. Keep the grafted part of the tree at least 2in (5cm) above the level of the soil. Firm the soil down gently with your feet and water in thoroughly. Keep the tree watered until it is established, feeding regularly. If growing against a wall, plant around 6–8in (15–20cm) away. Water plum trees thoroughly, avoiding waterlogging. In early spring, spread compost around the tree to a depth of up to 6in (15cm).

Plum trees won't produce fruit until year four or five, and harvesting lasts for around four weeks. Thin plums out to relieve stress on branches and to concentrate flavour and energy in smaller, higher-quality crops. Pick plums once they are easily removable, and discard any that are damaged and which will attract wasps and disease. Hang up 'wasp traps' (jars filled with sugary water) to prevent the theft of your fruit.

Prune when the fruiting period has ended. Cut away old, dead branches, maintaining the tree's shape, be it fan-trained against a wall, free-standing in a pyramid, a bush or standard tree. Pruning will also help to control silver leaf disease. Pull out mini-trees or 'suckers' which grow up from the roots. Don't prune when trees are dormant in winter. To deter overwintering pests, a horticultural oil-based winter wash can be applied in December or January. During the growing season, a lighter summer oil can be used, and protect from moths by applying a grease band 20in (50cm) above soil level.

Ripe plums are highly perishable but will last for a few days stored in a fridge. Under-ripe plums will ripen slowly if stored in a paper-lined box in a dark, cool environment.

# CHAPTER FOUR

# KEEPING ANIMALS

## CHICKENS

*The road to self-suffiency often starts with keeping chickens for fresh eggs.*

Here we are weighing up the pros and cons of keeping a small flock of chickens as a way of having your own supply of fresh eggs or even meat. Note that some of what is said about keeping a single chicken applies equally to a flock, while much of the advice on feeding and general care is also appropriate to both.

First of all, and this applies to one chicken or several, the keeping of chickens is not permitted everywhere, so it is advisable to check first with your local authority. In any case there are liable to be some restrictions, and you will most likely find that your chicken or chickens won't be allowed to range free but must be kept in a suitable enclosure; there may also be some kind of ruling as to how close to human dwellings such a structure may be sited.

Keeping chickens and raising chicks can be a rewarding experience.

## A Secure Place for Chickens

Many types of proprietary chicken housing systems are available, and there are plenty of companies around which can supply the items or even design and erect 'bespoke' housing especially for you. Have a look on the internet. In appearance, many typical proprietary systems are fairly similar to the type of structure often used for accommodating pet rabbits or guinea pigs outside. They are constructed of a wooden frame, which may be square or rectangular, usually with a side door for access. Other types may be triangular in cross-section, but in all cases the base of the run or pen is open to allow the birds to scratch and forage in the soil. One end of the pen includes the roost, which is a solid structure with a secure door and a waterproof top.

Unless you intend to let your chickens range freely, then an alternative system that works well is to keep them in a large, strongly-made and permanently-sited pen – usually made from wire mesh attached to a wooden frame – and to include within it, or as part of it, a sturdy, solid-sided but well-ventilated roosting place. The outer pen must have sufficiently high sides to prevent the chickens from escaping, and if possible be high enough to prevent cats and other animals from getting in; 5ft (1.6m) is the minimum for an open-topped run. A safer method is to have a relatively high-sided pen, with mesh covering the top as well, making it completely

secure. Such an enclosed system is regularly used by keepers of cagebirds that are housed outside. But in the end, the best way to deter marauding foxes is to install electric fencing or electrified netting.

Once erected, although the fencing around the pen may seem to be in good order, check it regularly for holes along the bottom; foxes may be trying to dig beneath the fencing to get in – a common and effective method used by them when trying to get into suburban gardens. It is best to ensure the bottom of the fencing extends a reasonable distance below ground (about 12in/30cm) to deter burrowing.

Make sure also that the gauge of the mesh is correct – if the holes are too large a chicken may get its head caught while trying to peck at something outside. Holes that are too large will also allow the opportunist paws of a would-be predator to grab an unsuspecting chicken; 0.5-in (about 13-mm) mesh is usually recommended. As a general rule, if you are to put your chickens in a covered run, with occasional access to the garden or some other free-range spot, a pen area of about 4ft² (0.4m²) per bird should be allowed, but if they are to be confined

Before buying chickens, make sure you have provided adequate fox-proof housing for them. Pictured opposite is an eglu, with a home-made chicken house on the right.

at all times, then allow more space per bird, in this case about 10ft² (0.9m²)

Like the pen, the chicken house or roost can be purchased ready-made, or you can erect one yourself, and there are plenty of books and websites that provide instructions. A typical roost is set slightly off the ground with a short ramp leading to the access door. It should be dry, draft-free but well-

ventilated. Make sure the roost is sited where there is shade, otherwise it may grow uncomfortably hot inside during the summer months.

The floor of the roost should be covered with clean straw laid on a thin layer of dust-free wood shavings, about an inch or two deep, which are readily available from pet supply stores and which should be changed regularly. Keep an eye on the 'bedding' to check for droppings, which must be removed every day. A removable droppings tray, placed beneath the roosting poles, will help to ensure that the area is kept clean and healthy. Soiled bedding makes good compost, so nothing need be wasted.

The roost must be cleared out weekly and fresh bedding laid down. Then, at least twice a year, but more often if conditions seem to dictate, the roost should be thoroughly stripped out and deep-cleaned. Everything should be removed, including bedding, nest boxes and any feeding containers. A safe cleaning agent should then be used to disinfect the walls, floor, roosting poles, and so on. Rinse everything with fresh water and leave to dry thoroughly before letting the chickens return, once fresh, clean bedding has been laid on the floor of the roost and in the nest box.

## Water and Food

Fresh drinking water must be available at all times when the chickens are in the pen. Under normal circumstances it is not necessary to provide water for them in the coop or roost as long as the birds are let out into the pen each morning to access drinking water for themselves. Various types of water dispensers are available, such as fountains which automatically fill up a trough with fresh water. Whatever type of water supply is used, make sure it is fixed at the recommended height and in accordance with the supplier's instructions. Don't use a water dispenser that might be fouled by the chickens hopping onto it. In cold weather, make sure that the water supply, or the reservoir, if one is fitted, is not allowed to freeze; chickens won't be able to survive for long without water. To make sure it remains ice-free, water can be brought into a warm place overnight and returned to the run the next morning.

Chickens require one of the good-quality proprietary complete pellet feeds that are available; this will ensure

OPPOSITE: These chickens are living within a large, well-fenced pen where there is space for foraging and a place to which they can retreat for the night.

RIGHT: An ideal night-time environment is a barn where there are plenty of high places where chickens can roost.

is worth providing a small container with an extra supply so that the chickens can take as much as they need.

Chickens also appreciate a little fresh greenery, so let them get onto grass as often as possible, or offer them plants to eat such as chickweed. Chickens are also happy to eat leftovers from the kitchen, but not, of course, as a substitute for properly designed chicken feed. They will eat fruit, cabbage, vegetable peelings, and so on. Do not, however, offer them anything strong-tasting such as onion, garlic or spices; neither should they be given citrus fruits (such as oranges and

they get a balanced diet of carbohydrate, fat and protein, vitamins and minerals (including calcium needed for eggshells). Use a commercially supplied dispenser or hopper for the pellets to prevent them from getting wet. A little grain can also be added, such as wheat or corn, to augment the diet if preferred, which can also be scattered around the pen area; most authorities advise this should be offered in the afternoon, with the pellet food given in the morning.

Grit is essential for many birds, not only chickens. Because they are without teeth, the abrasive properties of grit are needed in their crops (part of the digestive system) to help them grind up their food. Some grit should be present in good-quality proprietary feed, but it

lemons) nor any food in the process of 'going off'. Chickens shouldn't eat rotten food any more than we would ourselves; moreover, the likelihood is that it will be rejected and will be left to rot still further, eventually attracting vermin and flies.

## Egg-Laying

Even if you are keeping a single hen as a pet, she will reward you with eggs if you encourage her to lay. (Contrary to popular belief, a chicken will still lay eggs whether a rooster is present or not. The only difference is that without a male around to fertilize them the eggs will never produce chicks.) A nest box must be provided, raised a few inches off the ground within the roost; it should be lower than the highest roosting pole, however. Position the nest box in a quiet, dark place to help her feel more secure. Again, there is plenty of advice available in books and

OPPOSITE ABOVE: Chicken feeders allow just enough food through, keeping the remainder dry and rodent-free.

OPPOSITE BELOW: Fresh eggs for the table each morning is an appealing thought.

ABOVE: The Wyandotte chicken has most attractive plumage.

on the internet about how to create the ideal conditions for successful egg-laying. For example, it is possible to buy dummy eggs made from stone that encourage first layers to sit on their eggs without crushing them. (When young, I used to have great fun dropping these eggs in front of people, who didn't realize they were not real, just to see the shocked expression on their faces!)

The bottom of the nest should be lined with a little clean straw or pinewood shavings to help prevent the eggs from breaking when they are laid. (Despite all these measures, you will inevitably find broken eggs in the roost from time to time.)

### Obtaining Chickens

Once all the necessary accommodation and equipment is in place you can begin to think about obtaining birds and introducing them to their new home. At this point it is more than likely that you have made a decision concerning the type of chicken you want and why you want it; in other words, will it be essentially for eggs or for eating, will it be for showing or simply to be kept as a pet? You will need to consider the different types of chickens, their suitability from your point of view, their size, colour, temperament and hardiness. The more you can find out beforehand from other sources, including breeders and the

internet, the better. Seeing the actual breed in the flesh, moreover, is the best way of ensuring that you will ultimately be satisfied with your choice.

If you wish to keep chickens primarily for the quality of their eggs, then a commercial hybrid is the best choice. If you would prefer the eggs to be of a particular colour, then go for a pure breed. Wyandottes and Rhode Island Reds, for example, are among the breeds that lay mid-brown eggs, Leghorns lay white eggs, and Sussex hens tinted eggs, while Welsummers and Barnevelders lay dark-brown eggs, and those of Araucanas are blue. One of the drawbacks with hybrids is that they do not have the distinctive look of

OPPOSITE & BELOW: It is fortunate for those of us who enjoy her eggs that hens, given a little care and encouragement, are able to continue laying even when no rooster is present in the flock. A male will be needed, however, if the eggs are to be made fertile and eventually hatch to produce chicks.

some of the more spectacular breeds, but in their favour is the fact that they are cheaper to buy, come vaccinated against disease, and are excellent layers, some producing well in excess of 300 eggs in a year. Hybrids, of course, are the mainstay of the commercial industry for both meat and eggs.

Another route is to buy fertilized eggs and place them in an incubator until they hatch. This is particularly exciting for children, and there is the added benefit of seeing the chicks at the very earliest stages of their lives. If you are planning to try this, you must ensure that all the necessary equipment is in place before you obtain the eggs. There are plenty of books and websites that tell you how to set up an incubator, what the correct temperature should be, and what to do once the chicks have hatched (for

example, they need to be fed on chick starter feed for about six weeks, followed by a pullet feed). You will also be warned to make sure that the chicks are kept safe from another form of predator – in this case the pet cat or dog – which may be tempted to eat a small chick sitting in a warm box in the house!

Ex-battery hens, which have reached the end of their commercial life – usually at about 72 weeks – are fast becoming another choice for the amateur chicken-keeper or for those who want a bird or a number of birds that they can keep on a small scale. There are several organizations that specialize in rescuing these hens and offering them to people willing to give them a new life. It can be an initially sad yet ultimately rewarding experience to take on one of these birds. Some of them will be traumatized and even in bad condition to begin with; they may have poor feathering, and may even need to regrow their beaks. But just as with other rescue animals, such as cats and dogs, with the proper care and attention there is no reason why they should not, in time, return to their full vigour and fine appearance.

### Keeping Chickens Healthy

Chickens are pretty robust and healthy most of the time, but they can succumb to illness and disease like any other animal. Chickens kept in flocks can quickly transmit diseases to others, which will compound the initial problem. If detected early enough, however, most ailments can be treated. Before this happens, however, it is worth acquainting yourself with details of a vet in your area who is skilled in avian (bird) medicine. Ask your local vet if he can provide such a service, and if not, ask him to recommend another who can. Your local authority or pet rescue centre may also be able to offer

Check your chickens regularly for signs and symptoms of disease.

advice, since they may themselves call upon veterinary services from time to time. Symptoms of disease can manifest

themselves in various ways, so it is sensible to check each bird daily to make sure they are not presenting any early symptoms. Look in particular for the following:

• Listlessness or loss of appetite – does the chicken seem to be behaving differently from normal?
• Poor feather condition – feathers should appear sleek and 'well-groomed' in a healthy bird. Do not confuse poor feather condition with moulting, which all birds undergo to replace their feathers as part of the natural cycle. Egg-laying will also be curtailed during the moulting period.
• Any obvious change in the pecking order; if you have more than one chicken, is the one in question being bullied or dominated by one normally lower in rank?
• Sneezing.
• Parasites on the feathers or skin, or a generally 'mangy' appearance.
• Unusual-looking stools (droppings) and/or the appearance in the stools of worms; normal stools are brownish with a white 'cap'.

It must be stressed, however, that these are not the only signs of illness, and if you have any other reasons to suspect that not all is well, expert advice should be sought as soon as possible.

Many diseases may be encouraged by poor hygiene regimes in the coop, so be sure that the cleaning procedures, described earlier, are followed scrupulously at all times.

In addition to dealing with illnesses, there are a number of measures that should be taken so that your chickens remain healthy. These include preventing worms or dealing with them once their presence has been detected.

There are several types of parasitic worm of which the most common is the roundworm. Tapeworms are less commonly problematical but are still a cause for concern, and similar symptoms as those shown by roundworm infestation are often seen. In cases of worm infestation, or to prevent worms in the first place, an anti-worming treatment is advised. This should be carried out at least twice yearly, or according to your vet's instructions. During the treatment, and for a period following it, none of the affected chicken's eggs must be consumed.

The beaks of birds grow continually, as do our own fingernails, this constant growth being an important factor that repairs normal wear and tear. Chickens that range freely tend to keep their own beaks in trim through the abrasive action of pecking around in the soil. It is possible that the upper

LEFT: To avoid disease, keep coops clean and disinfected and regularly change soiled bedding.

OPPOSITE: Check beaks and claws to see if they need to be clipped.

mandible (the top part of the beak) will sometimes overgrow the lower one if the chicken is not allowed to feed in this manner – for example, if the food is too soft and the conditions for general pecking and foraging are not met. If the beak does overgrow in this way, it must be trimmed back, otherwise the chicken will not be able to eat and drink normally. Experienced chicken-keepers often do this job themselves, but initially it is advisable to have a vet or similarly qualified person do it for you so that you may see for yourself how it is done.

Claws may also need trimming, since they grow in the same way as beaks. Again, in ideal conditions, all the scratching at the ground, which a chicken does in the normal course of finding food, will tend to keep the claws at the correct length; but if they get too long – usually as a result of walking on soft litter – then they will need to be cut back, otherwise foot problems can ensue. Like the beak, this is a job you can do yourself, but to begin with, a 'lesson' from an experienced person is required.

Some chickens are born with defects, such as a beak that is twisted to the left or right instead of growing straight. There may also be a visible gap between the upper and lower mandibles when the mouth is closed. Such conditions can affect a bird's ability to feed properly, and special foods may be required. Unless caused by an injury,

defects of this type are usually genetic in origin and it is best not to use such birds for breeding to avoid passing the condition on to the next generation.

External parasites, such as lice and mites, can also be a problem. Lice are easier to spot than mites, since they are bigger; they may be seen around the

bases of the feathers and their eggs are visibly attached to them. Look particularly around the vent and under the wings where the softer downy feathers grow. Dust baths help chickens get rid of lice naturally, but special treatments are also available to rid them of these troublesome parasites.

## DUCKS

*There are many advantages in keeping ducks; they will provide you with eggs, they are an excellent form of pest control and their antics are particularly amusing to watch.*

Keeping ducks in a backyard is much easier than you would expect. They need a little more space than chickens, in terms of run and coop size, and a few little extras to keep them healthy and happy, but you will be amply rewarded for any extra work that may be involved.

ABOVE & RIGHT: Decorative duck houses can be a cheerful addition to any pond, and placed in the centre will offer protection from predators.

OPPOSITE: Ducks like to roam free to graze.

### Shelter and Protection

Ducks are sociable creatures and it is recommended that at least two are kept to avoid boredom and loneliness. While ducks might prefer being outside for most of the time, they also like a place to which they can retreat at times to rest and preen their feathers. Like chickens, however, they are a target for foxes, and every night must be safely

118

perfectly acceptable to feed domestic ducks chicken layers pellets which have the right concentrations of protein (16–18%), calcium (2–3%), carbohydrates, fibre (6%), Omega 3 oils (4%), vitamins and minerals. Ducks are also good at foraging for plant material, such as seeds, grains, acorns, grass shoots and also insects, snails and slugs and aquatic invertebrates.

locked in a building or secure fenced-off area to minimize the risk of predatory attacks. Housing must be large enough to provide each duck with at least 3–4ft$^2$ of floor space. The accommodation can be as basic or as elaborate as you wish as long as the birds are given the shade and protection they need, and that it is kept clean and dry with adequate bedding and ventilation.

## Feeding

Ducks are incredibly hardy and adaptable, but for optimum health and to help them produce eggs they need the correct balance of nutrients. It is

OPPOSITE: Ducks, though hardy creatures, will require some shade and protection.

RIGHT: Ducks need water and a pond is ideal. If this is not possible, however, then provide them with a children's paddling pool, making sure it is cleaned out regularly.

## Water

Ducks enjoy water and there is nothing nicer that to see them swimming about in a pool, provided the water is not stagnant. But even without one it is still possible to keep the smaller domestic ducks happy with a tub that is emptied and refilled daily with fresh water. They must also have a reasonable amount of space and most of all grass to eat. It is also essential to a duck's health and well-being that it has a constant supply of fresh water, not only to drink but in which to clean its eyes and nostrils.

Drinking vessels must be cleaned regularly to remove the build-up of harmful bacteria, and the water must be replaced every couple of days. In very cold weather, make sure that the water has not turned to ice, thus preventing the duck from drinking.

Like all animals, ducks may become unwell from time to time, so it is important that their behaviour is observed and that they are physically checked, with any health concerns reported to your vet.

## Health

Keeping ducks healthy requires taking the necessary steps to prevent disease outbreaks in the first place. If your ducks seem unwell, but there is no obvious sign of injury or disease, then it may be that their diet is the problem. First check that they aren't eating any poisonous plants. Second, you could try changing to a different feed. Third, check their gullets; ducks like to forage, so there is the risk of them picking up dangerous objects which can become stuck in their gullets. This can result in gradual weight loss, lethargy and eventually death. Don't allow your ducks to drink or clean themselves in dirty water. Don't give them feed that is old or damp, and never pick them up by their legs or feet.

If in any doubt concerning a health issue, contact your vet at once.

## GEESE

*Geese make excellent 'guard dogs' besides providing fresh eggs and meat.*

Geese appear to be out of fashion at the moment, having a reputation of being somewhat aggressive; but they do not bite unless scared or provoked. They will act as natural lawn mowers, however, and provide you with delicious free-range eggs to eat. Geese have excellent eyesight and make good burglar alarms. They can be relied upon to warn of the approach of intruders.

### Feeding

Geese are fairly self-sufficient, and if there is a good supply of grass available, then they won't need much additional feeding; but if grass is in short supply, they can be fed other greenery, such as lettuce or cabbage. A good quality geese feed or small grain,

RIGHT: Geese are essentially grazers, so a good supply of grass is important. Their diet can be supplemented, however, with grain and green vegetables.

OPPOSITE: Geese enjoy swimming, though a pond is not essential.

124

such as corn, barley and soybeans, can be used when grass is in short supply.

Geese love foraging and should be provided with an area which they can graze surrounded by a 3-ft fence to prevent them from straying and predators from entering. Be aware that geese will eat anything, so protect trees and plants with nets or fencing. Geese should also be given access to flint grit to aid digestion.

## Shelter

Geese do not require anything elaborate by way of accommodation, and a movable shed with a flat, sloping roof would make a suitable shelter. The shed needs to be completely enclosed and locked at night for protection against foxes, dogs etc, while a thin layer of wood shavings or sawdust on the floor will make cleaning easier. Geese tend to foul their sleeping quarters so damp litter must be removed frequently.

## Health

Check geese regularly for signs of disease such as loss of condition, consulting your vet if in any doubt.

Vermin cause a myriad of problems in that they are attracted by the presence of food and can transmit disease, cause damage and in some cases attack goslings. The best approach is to try to deter them as far as possible and consult a professional if poison is to be used. Remember to
• Clear up spilt food
• Keep feed in vermin-proof containers
• Block up holes in sheds where vermin may enter

OPPOSITE LEFT: The goose has a raucous voice and will sound the alert when strangers approach.

OPPOSITE RIGHT: Check geese daily for signs of disease and consult your vet if anything seems to be amiss.

ABOVE RIGHT: White and grey Sebastopol goslings.

RIGHT: Geese like to graze together in flocks.

## TURKEYS

*Keeping turkeys as pets or for meat is becoming increasingly popular. Turkeys are fascinating birds, being very decorative and relatively easy to rear.*

Turkeys grow to be large birds that are mostly docile but they can be aggressive during the breeding season. They are actually quite intelligent animals, have their own individual personalities, and require little grooming. But if you are considering keeping them, then you should know that they do have some special requirements when it comes to housing and feeding.

Of relative importance is the fact that a domestic male can mature at a

massive 86lbs (39kg), which is about four times that of a wild turkey. Males grow to be 4ft (1.2m) long with females about 12in shorter. Wingspan can be as much as 6ft.

Some domestic turkeys are able to fly while others are not. It is believed that they can move at 35mph (56km/h), when required, but have worse hearing and eyesight than their wild cousins. Females communicate, making their well-known clucking sound, while males will fascinate you with their gobble-gobbles. Interestingly, only the males can put on a show by fanning out their tail feathers, a talent the females do not share.

## Shelter

For overnight use, half a dozen turkeys may be housed in a good-quality 8 x 6ft garden shed. Good ventilation is required, and a 3-in pole placed about 2$^{1}$/2ft off the ground will make an acceptable perch. The shed must be kept clean at all times, with the waste material raked out and new hay or straw laid down. It is essential that

OPPOSITE LEFT: Turkeys are striking birds with the potential to grow impressively large.

OPPOSITE RIGHT: A male Bourbon Red displaying his tail feathers.

RIGHT: A Black Spanish male.

turkeys are kept safely locked away at night when foxes are abroad and on the prowl.

You will also need to create a fenced-in area to protect the birds when they are foraging outside. This must be at least 6ft (2m) high, though it is still possible for hen turkeys to fly over and out if they have a mind to do so. Mostly, however, they are well-behaved, particularly if there is sufficient vegetation to keep them interested.

## Feeding

Much of the turkeys' diet will be in the form of pellets, but they also love vegetables, fruits, weeds, leaves, acorns, nuts, grapes, grass, kale and berries, while on occasion they will also eat oatmeal, cracked chicken eggs, insects and even small animals that may find their way into the pen.

Some young turkey will not accept pellets at first so you may need to feed them crickets, spiders, earthworms, meal worms and beetles that you can catch yourself or purchase at pet stores. It is important, if you catch this kind of live food yourself, to be sure that they have not been exposed to insecticides.

Crushed oyster shells, added to the feed, are an excellent source of calcium. Turkeys also need grit to enable them to grind up their food in their gizzards. This should be provided at all times or the birds will be unable to digest their food properly. Fresh water must always

be made available, ideally in a special poultry water dispenser.

## General Care

It is important that turkeys are provided with sufficient space in which to exercise. When cared for properly, their life expectancy is around 12 years, but overfeeding and inadequate exercise exposes them to the danger of becoming too large to carry their own body weight.

Domestic turkeys are prone to blackhead disease, caused by a microscopic protozoan called *Histomonas meleagridis*, which is a dangerous parasite. While domestic chickens are not so affected they can

carry the parasite and pass it on to turkeys. Blackhead causes the livers of turkeys to become enlarged and is generally fatal.

## PIGS

*Pigs are often near to the top of the list when it comes to keeping free-range livestock on a small scale.*

Pigs will eat almost anything they are given, and can even digest grass, though they will not thrive on this alone. They will also convert virtually

OPPOSITE: A domesticated turkey.

ABOVE: Young poultry are called poults.

everything you grow into the most delicious meat and byproducts. And while they may not be everyone's idea of the perfect pet, the fact that they are such pleasant, cheerful and intelligent creatures makes them a pleasure to have around.

### Before Starting
Rushing headlong into pig-keeping, without considering all the implications, is a recipe for disaster. Pigs need to be housed properly and they need space in which to run around. They will also churn up your land, and may even eat you out of house and home. Remember that even though they may start out small and adorable, they will grow to be very large indeed. Like all animals, pigs get sick and eventually die and, if not used for meat, may live for 20 years, making them very long-term commitments indeed.

You would be well-advised to enrol yourself in one of the many excellent courses on pig-keeping that are becoming increasingly available. These offer fun introductions to the subject, allowing you to handle the animals while gathering valuable information and advice. They will also help you get to grips with the paperwork and legal side of keeping pigs. You must also check government guidelines and legislation, much of which needs sorting out even before

you buy your pigs, and which must be followed whether you have just one pig or several.

### Making a Choice
Some will opt for one of the rarer breeds, not only with the idea of saving them from extinction, but also

BELOW: A Tamworth sow.

OPPOSITE: Before buying a pig, think long and hard. Piglets, when small, are very appealing, but they will eventually grow to be very large animals indeed.

because it is considered that they produce tastier meat. Popular American breeds from which to choose are: Duroc, American Landrace and Yorkshire, while others include Berkshire, British Lop, British Saddleback, Gloucestershire Old Spot, Large Black, Middle White, Tamworth and Welsh. The American Livestock Breed Conservancy and the British Rare Breeds Survival Trust are excellent sources of information. Each breed has its own characteristics and it is important to match it to the

BELOW: Some prefer to raise rare-breed pigs as a way of preserving the breed. This is a Gloucestershire Old Spot.

OPPOSITE: A Large Black sow and her piglets. The American Livestock Breeds Conservancy has added this breed to the 'critical' list.

type of land on which it will live. It may also be worthwhile seeking out others who keep pigs in your area, in the hope that their intimate knowledge of a particular breed might prove to be of interest and particular value to you.

Buying Pigs
When acquiring pigs, it is important to make sure they come from a reputable breeder, and the various associations and societies, that concern themselves with particular breeds, will advise you accordingly.

Keeping pigs outdoors presents a number of problems, including 'heat stress', because they have no sweat glands with which to naturally cool themselves. Therefore pigs require access to water or a 'wallow', which is an area of mud, otherwise they will roll in their own excrement, which they would not normally do. Ideally, a cement wallow, which contains water, cools the pigs much better, although mud serves to protect light-coloured pigs from sunburn. It is also important that shade is provided. Remember that pigs are rooting animals and voracious feeders, and will strip every plant in their vicinity. They will soon make a 'mess' of their pen, which belies the fact that, contrary to popular belief, they are actually clean animals.

## Shelter

Somewhere will also be needed to accommodate them. Pig arks are suitable for this purpose and are readily available, these being triangular structures raised off the ground to ensure the animals remain dry. The pigs will need plenty of straw, and some form of fencing to keep them on their own patch and out of yours. Electric fencing works well for this purpose, but wooden post-and-rail is easier on the eye if the pen is to be in full view of your house.

BELOW: If you keep your pigs outside you will need to provide them with adequate shelter from the elements.

OPPOSITE: Pigs do not sweat and consequently need to wallow in mud to cool themselves down.

# KEEPING ANIMALS

LEFT: Make sure pigs are securely penned in when left outside.

BELOW: Pig need are dry place off the ground, with plenty of clean bedding to lie on.

OPPOSITE: Light-skinned pigs, in particular, must be provided with shade to protect them from sunburn.

idea, do not feed them meat, which is illegal in many countries.

## Health
Remember that not all vets are willing to accept pigs as patients, so it's worth checking this out in the early stages

## Feeding
Pigs are non-ruminants with a single stomach, unlike animals such as cattle and goats. To grow rapidly and efficiently they need a high-energy, concentrated grain diet that is low in fibre (cellulose) and which is supplemented with adequate protein.

One-half to two-thirds of a pig's body is made up of water, making it the most important part of its diet. Therefore it should be supplied with as much clean, fresh water as it will drink. Be careful not to overfeed your animals and, while giving them scraps from the kitchen and garden is a good

and not waiting for an emergency to strike. Pigs tend to stay relatively fit, because of the foraging they do, but it is worth getting them used to being stroked and handled, which will make life easier should they need to be examined by a vet. It will also make keeping pigs that bit more enjoyable for you.

## COWS

*Cows occupy a unique role in human history, having been domesticated since at least the early Neolithic period.*

Cows are ruminants, meaning they have a digestive system that allows otherwise indigestible food to be consumed, by repeatedly regurgitating and rechewing it as 'cud'. Cattle are raised for meat (beef cattle), dairy products and hides.

Keeping livestock of any kind is a big responsibility and should never be taken lightly. Before getting a cow of your own, consider borrowing one for a week or so to see what is involved and how it will affect your own daily routine.

There are many benefits to keeping a cow, the main one being that a daily supply of fresh, unpasteurised milk and cream will be readily available to turn into butter and cheese. A little additional income can also be generated from the produce.

You will need to feed and milk your cow every morning and night, at 12-hourly intervals. She will need to be mated with a bull once a year to make her pregnant so that she keeps on producing milk. You must then raise

RIGHT: A cow needs to have a calf once a year in order to produce milk.

OPPOSITE: At least one acre of pasture is needed per cow.

OPPOSITE: The keeping of rare breeds has become more popular in recent years. These are Highland cattle.

BELOW: Dexters are small, short-legged cattle that originated in Ireland.

the young calf and either keep it or sell it on at market.

Keeping a cow will also entail butter- and cheese-making, growing and harvesting hay and sugar beet to feed your cow, and grooming, cleaning and mucking out of barns.

### Making a Choice

Jersey cows are often the first choice because they are small and produce rich milk. They are also said to make good pets. Whatever the breed, it is a good idea to get the same breed as other farmers in your locality, so that when it comes to mating your cow there will be a suitable bull available.

### Buying Cows

When buying a cow, choose the healthiest one possible (you will need a vet to check her over). Make sure she

It is important that the barn has its own supply of running water, both for the cow to drink and for cleaning purposes.

It is also worth keeping a three-bin compost system nearby, so that well-rotted manure is always available for use on your vegetable patch.

At least one acre of land is required per cow, divided into three separate pastures which the cow can graze in rotation and where you can grow and harvest your own hay.

General milking equipment will include a milk pail, water pail, milking stool, manure shovel and fork, halter and rope, comb and brush, barn thermometer, udder washcloths, milk scale, hay forks and a wheelbarrow. You may also wish to invest in a milk churn, in which to make butter, as well as cheese-making equipment.

has been tested for tuberculosis and check her udders for signs of mastitis. Examine milking records to ensure she produces a good yield.

Once the initial cost of buying a cow has been found, and all the necessary equipment bought, there should be very few other outgoings. By growing and harvesting your own hay, moreover, there will be little need to feed her with grain, which only leaves further outlay for possible veterinary treatment and the purchase of additional bedding for use in the barn during the winter months.

### Shelter & Equipment
Some basic equipment needs to be bought once the decision has been made. The first item to consider is a barn that will accommodate your cow in winter. This must be comfortable and draft-free and ideally have a window to let in plenty of sunlight and fresh air. Storage will also be required for the bales of hay needed to feed her in the winter. Less space will be required if you decide to buy hay by the bale, but rather more storage will be needed if you intend to produce your own hay.

### Feeding & Health
During the spring, summer and autumn months, cows return to the fields after milking. Grass is the cheapest form of food, and well-managed herds are able to produce large quantities of milk from it.

ABOVE LEFT: In winter, when the weather gets cold, cows should be brought into the barn and fed hay, grain and water.

OPPOSITE: Regularly check your cows for signs of disease.

The most important consideration is to keep your cow, and her milk, healthy. Keep her out on pasture until the cold winter months, then give her all the quality hay she needs, to which may be added a half-pound or so of grain while milking, with a vitamin-mineral supplement as extra insurance. Silage is also a valuable food; this is a form of pickling that preserves summer grass for use during the leaner winter months. A salt block to lick on should also be provided, also plenty of fresh water.

Mastitis and lameness are the most common adverse conditions affecting cows, and a vet must be called at once if these or any other types of disease are suspected.

## GOATS

*Goats have grown more popular in recent years because of the health benefits of their milk.*

Goats have had something of a bad reputation for centuries. Not only were they long associated with satanists and the devil, but we are also warned of their habit of springing an attack any time our backs are turned. But the reality is very different; in fact goats are charming animals with a great deal of character. According to the ancient Greeks, the Capricorn of the zodiac was sexy, lively and health-giving. The females do not smell, if looked after properly, and the milk, besides tasting good, is easier to digest than cow's, can be tolerated by people with allergies, and makes excellent cheese.

Goats are in many ways the ideal choice for the smallholder, but they are not to be compared with sheep, being sociable and capable of forming complex relationships with others in their herd. For this reason it would be unkind to keep one goat on its own.

RIGHT: Goats require a large pen with a high fence. Give them something to climb onto, however, to keep them happy and active.

OPPOSITE: The Golden Guernsey is an efficient milk-producer for its relatively small size.

## Making a Choice

All females that have produced kids should give milk, but some breeds give more than others, and selection processes have resulted in a number of breeds that are kept largely for milk production, Swiss breeds being the most prolific where this is concerned. There are also breeds that are kept specifically for meat, such as the Boer, while others, such as the Turkish Angora, are kept for their fleece.

## Shelter

A dry, draft-free building is required, with shelter from the elements and sufficient headroom for the animal to stand upright on its hindlegs with neck outstretched. Good ventilation and natural lighting are essential, but all windows must be protected from goat damage. The floor area, where the goat lies down, must be draft-free. If penned separately, each goat must have about 44ft$^2$ (4m$^2$) of floor space. Goats like to see one another, even if penned separately, so provision needs to be made to accommodate this.

A well-fenced exercise yard is required that is at least three to four times the area of the pen. This needs to be concreted or have a similar hard surface that does not retain moisture and that can be easily cleaned. Otherwise goats can be turned out to graze/browse in a well-fenced paddock during the day in all but very bad

weather. Field shelters are appreciated.

Horned and disbudded or hornless goats must be penned separately.

A dry area is needed in which to store straw, hay and other feed. Protect it from damp, contamination and vermin. A nearby supply of fresh water is also required, as is a clean area for milking should you have a dairy goat.

## Feeding

Left to their own devices, goats wander about taking a little of this and something of that. They find hedgerows particularly attractive. Good hay is the single most important item of diet. At least half the diet (on a dry weight basis) should consist of forage. Green food, concentrates, minerals, vitamins and water are also important, and a balanced and adequate diet is crucial to good health. Any change to the diet must be made gradually to enable the rumen bacteria to adjust. Other suitable foods are a good-quality goat mix and sugar-beet pulp.

OPPOSITE: The angora goat is largely bred for its fleece (mohair).

RIGHT:
Female goats are one of those rare animals that sometimes produce milk without being pregnant, although offspring are produced in the usual way with the help of a male; you will need to decide whether to keep the kids or sell them on once they are born.

Individual pens need hayracks, feed and water buckets and bucket-holders. Feed and hay are usually placed outside pens, allowing the goats to feed through slatted barriers. To prevent bullying there should be a sufficient number of openings in the slats for all to feed at the same time. Salt licks must be provided at all times.

## Health

Good health can only be achieved as part of general good management, which includes adequate housing, exercise and feeding, the prevention and treatment of parasitic worm infestations being particularly important.

Close observation of your goats is essential if you are to learn what is 'normal' and what is not. Since some conditions have gradual onsets, being able to spot symptoms should enable you to act promptly and prevent risk to other animals in the vicinity.

Males may become sexually active when only a few weeks old, which

OPPOSITE: The Toggenburg is named after the region in Switzerland where the breed originated.

RIGHT: Goats, being hardy creatures, require minimal shade and shelter during the summer months. Sturdier accommodation is needed in winter, however, and for females ready to give birth.

means they must be kept separate from females from about six weeks of age to avoid accidents. Males are used for stud purposes in their first autumn, although late-born kids may not be ready until later in the breeding season.

## SHEEP

*There are good reasons for keeping sheep: they provide fine fleeces, delicious meat, and are great at cropping grass and keeping it short. But you'll need to be adequately prepared.*

### Making a Choice

Different breeds of sheep thrive on different types of grazing, so it is recommended that you speak to local farmers and discover which animals best suits the environment. There are more breed types of sheep than any other farm animal, so there are plenty from which to choose.

Lush pastureland will accommodate around four to five sheep per acre, so plan numbers accordingly, remembering that it is better to have too few sheep rather than too many.

### Buying Sheep

Once you've decided how many sheep (and which kind) you want, there are two main choices: either find a farmer who breeds sheep for sale, or head for market. If possible, a private purchase

LEFT & ABOVE: Keeping rare-breed sheep has become popular in recent years and their fleeces can be quite valuable.

OPPOSITE: A ewe and her lamb in an idyllic setting. Remember, however, that sheep require a good deal of care and attention.

from a reputable breeder is the best option, in which case the breeder should be able to give you valuable advice, and you can study the sheep in your own time in open fields. The sheeps' medical and family history can also be obtained at the same time.

Market purchases can be cheaper, but sheep bought in this manner come into contact with many others of their kind along the way, and disease can spread as a result.

Make sure to obtain the relevant paperwork to enable you to keep sheep

ABOVE: In summer, sheep are content with grass and weeds, but hay and grain must be added to their diet in winter.

OPPOSITE: An acre of lush pasture will support four to five sheep.

on your own land. Legislation varies throughout the world and your property may need to be registered as an 'agricultural holding'.

Record-keeping may also be mandatory, with regulations governing the movement of livestock strictly adhered to at all times. You should contact your local US Department of Food and Agriculture for more information regarding the legalities of keeping sheep in the USA, or visit the DEFRA website if you live in Britain.

Feeding

Sheep are content with grass, weeds and water for most of the year. Indeed, one of the reasons why they are so popular is that they help to keep fields from becoming overgrown. In winter, however, when

Fortunately, sheep are fairly hardy, and diseases can be minimized if they are kept in good conditions, with well-ventilated housing and rotated between different areas of grass. Good hygiene starts with ensuring that hooves and wool are kept clear of faecal matter, in which flies and other insects are likely to lay their larvae, and which go on to eat into the flesh of the sheep.

Diseases of the hooves include paratuberculosis and foot and mouth, when it is vital to separate affected animals from the rest of the herd. Sheep are also subject to scab, diarrhoea (scour), ticks, lice, fleas, orf, fly strike and pasteurella. Lameness and foot problems being fairly common, it is important to inspect feet regularly. It is also necessary to trim the feet from time to time, depending on the terrain on which the sheep are kept.

Kept outside, sheep will naturally segregate the areas where they defecate and rest, and space must be allowed to accommodate this. Pens must be washed out every day, if necessary, and sheep should be given an antiseptic bath at least once a week. Netting pens will also offer some defence from flies and midges.

Shearing generally takes place in spring, as the fleece starts to lift. This helps to prevent overheating during warmer summer temperatures, and also makes it easier for lambs to feed.

the ground is frost-hardened and the grass is short of nutrients, it will be necessary to supplement their diet with hay and grain. If only a few sheep are involved, give them a handful of

ABOVE: Sheep are usually sheared in the spring to prevent them from becoming overheated during the warmer months. The fleece can be sold, the value of it depending on the quality and condition of the wool.

OPPOSITE: Control disease by rotating pasture at intervals, maintaining clean living environments and checking stock regularly for pests and diseases.

'sheep nuts' from a bucket each day. This routine helps to train the sheep, eventually allowing you to manoeuvre them without help from a sheepdog.

## Health

Sheep are probably the most susceptible of all livestock to infections and infestations that can either affect productivity or kill the animals altogether. The existence of insect vectors means that a clean environment is important; diseases can also be transmitted through faeces and from close contact with other animals that have become infected.

## HORSES

*Today, horses and ponies tend to be kept for equestrian pursuits rather than as working animals, as was once the case. But there are ways of making money from horses, such as breeding them or renting land and accommodation to other horse-owners. You might also offer a full livery service, with stabling, schooling arenas and jumps, etc.*

### Making a Choice

It is important, before buying a horse, to consider not only the expenses involved in actually buying one but also the costs of keeping it. When choosing an animal make sure it fits the requirements of your lifestyle. If you require a horse to work the land, for instance, choose a heavy breed or cob type. For many, however, keeping a

If, exceptionally, you wish to use horses to work your land, choose from the heavier breeds such as the ones pictured here. Heavy horses are also much hardier than the lighter breeds.

horse is solely for the pleasure of riding it, but remember that Thoroughbreds and warmbloods will require stabling and generally more care than the hardy native breeds.

## Accommodation

Horses are grazing animals and all should be turned out in a field for at least part of the day. The rule is approximately an acre of land per horse. The grazing land must be well-fenced with a fresh water supply. Droppings should be removed daily to prevent the grass from becoming 'sour' and inedible. Horses and ponies

OPPOSITE: An acre of land per horse is the minimum requirement.

RIGHT: Sturdy fences are a necessity, with post and rail the safest though the most expensive.

which are to live out all-year-round must be provided with a well-constructed field shelter.

Most people prefer to keep their horses in at night, particularly in the winter, and a well-ventilated, roomy stall or stable should be supplied. It must be of sturdy construction, the entrance facing away from prevailing winds. Some horses are kept in large barns which are divided into stalls.

## Feeding

The horse's natural diet is the grass and herbs found in pasture. In warm months, when the grass is abundant,

OPPOSITE & ABOVE: Stables must be draft-free but well-ventilated. Horses should be supplied with hay, feed and water and be cleaned out daily (twice daily if the animals live in).

they can survive on little else, although they may require supplementary feeding for optimum health in drought conditions or in winter, consisting of cereals and hay. These days, many feeds come ready-mixed and designed for horses in various stages of work. Make sure that plenty of fresh water is always made available.

## Health

Great care and attention must be taken to make sure your horse keeps healthy. Your vet will provide yearly jabs to protect against equine diseases, and will also check the animal's heart, lungs and eyes to ensure they are working properly. Regular care of the hooves is vital: the farrier should visit every six to eight weeks to trim hooves and fit new shoes if required.

A yearly dental check is also advised; this is because a horse's teeth continue to grow and often develop rough edges which cause discomfort when eating. It is also important that tack and rugs are correctly fitted as ill-fitting equipment is liable to cause great discomfort.

RIGHT: A visit from the farrier will be required every six to eight weeks to check that new shoes are not needed and that feet are in good condition.

OPPOSITE: Regular worming is essential, particularly for mares in foal. Seek vet advice.

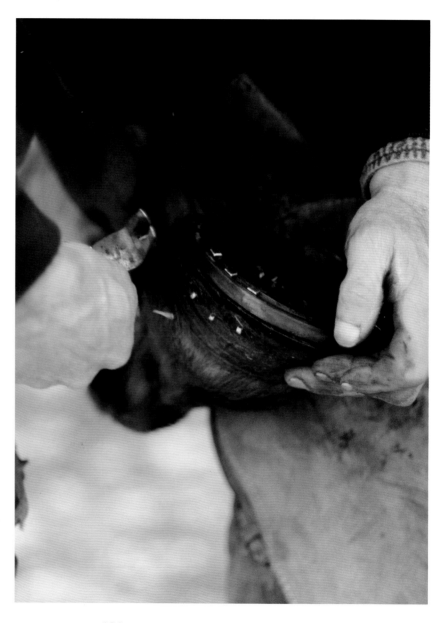

## ALPACAS

*Alpacas are environmentally friendly animals that are easy to keep and lovely to behold.*

Related to the llama, another herd animal, alpacas are naturally curious, docile and friendly, and can be very affectionate when handled correctly. They make excellent companions for other animals, such as horses, sheep, goats and even chickens. Alpaca fleece is incredibly soft and light, widely sought for its luxurious feel and durable quality. It is naturally hypoallergenic and much lighter, warmer and less itchy than sheeps' wool. The fibre is also popular for homespinning, or it can be sent to specialist processors to be turned into fabric or knitting yarns.

### Making a Choice

Alpacas come in a wide range of colours – from white, fawns, browns and greys through to black and multi-colours. They communicate particularly through tail and ear positions and by emitting a range of curious humming sounds.

RIGHT: Alpacas are charming animals, valued for their soft and luxurious fleeces.

OPPOSITE: As herding animals, alpacas are only happy when kept in groups.

It is a good sign if an alpaca looks healthy and cared-for. But you will also need to check vaccination and worming records, and whether or not the animal is registered, in which case its parentage and pedigree can also be checked.

## Shelter

It is important to remember that alpacas are herd animals and will live happier, healthier lives if they have the company of at least one other of their own kind, preferably two. Up to six alpacas can be kept on an acre of land, in which case hand-feeding at various times throughout the year may be required, depending on the quality of the pasture. A pair of gelded males or a pair of females would be ideal and are easily cared for by beginners.

## Feeding

Alpacas are hardy animals, and feeding with hay or alpaca pellets is only necessary if the pasture is sparse or overgrazed; the animals are keen grazers and browsers and will tackle bark or leaves, so it is wise to fence off young shrubs or trees. It is important that a source of water be made available to them at all times.

Alpacas can be given a daily vitamin/mineral supplement, which also helps with training, and pregnant females and youngsters should also have extra protein feeds. Extra hay can be given in winter.

## Health

Alpacas like plenty of attention but minimal care to keep them healthy and happy, and they are normally vaccinated and wormed twice a year. Their toenails are trimmed two or three times a year, and their four large front teeth may need trimming once a year, which is easiest done when the shearer comes to call.

Diet and nutrition have a bearing on the fineness and density of an alpaca's fleece, and animals that are overfed will produce fleeces with a higher (coarser) micron count than those on a properly balanced diet. Drastic changes of diet, or high levels of stress, will directly affect the quality of the fibre produced by the animal at that time.

LEFT: Correct feeding is important for good health and will be reflected in the quality of the fleece.

OPPOSITE: Have alpacas professionally sheared once a year, taking the opportunity to have their toenails and teeth trimmed at the same time.

# CHAPTER FIVE

# KEEPING BEES

*Bees are held in high regard, due to their usefulness as pollinators and as producers of honey, their social nature, and their reputation for diligence.*

## The Right Choice?

Bee-keeping won't suit everyone: although keeping bees does not require the sort of stamina or time needed to look after, say, horses or some other livestock, it nevertheless calls for certain things to be done at certain times. Emergencies or potential problems must be dealt with promptly, taking the right course of action, and the whole enterprise needs to be set up and maintained correctly to ensure a happy and successful hive. Remember, you are working with live creatures that will depend, to some extent, on you for their health and well-being.

## Making a Start

Before going to the trouble and expense of getting the bees for your hive and buying all the necessary equipment – and indeed, there is plenty of it on offer to tempt the unwary – it is worth

attending demonstrations, such as those often held by local bee-keeping associations. Here you will see exactly what is involved in opening the hive and handling the bees, and there will, of course, be opportunities to ask knowledgeable and experienced bee-keepers to answer the questions that have been bothering you.

OPPOSITE: Before getting some bees of your own, why not attend bee-keeping classes?

ABOVE: Site the hives in a sunny position but where there is shelter from the wind.

It is necessary to consider the best place in which to position a hive before you purchase any equipment, and then set about preparing the site in anticipation of its arrival. It goes without saying that the hive should be placed on firm, dry, weed-free ground. A well-ventilated sunny aspect is also ideal, perhaps one that faces south or east. Locate the hive away from frost pockets, areas of damp and wind, if possible. Remember that you will need comfortable access to the hive yourself, and a hive stand will make the task that much easier; some hives come with legs

already attached and these may give you all the height you need. The stand must be tall enough to keep the hive out of reach of marauding animals and strong enough to support the weight of a healthy colony, which may eventually reach about 150lbs (70kg) or so.

Fresh water must be available at all times; if there is no natural source of water close by, then one must be provided. This can be a moderately large, shallow dish sited off the ground, a shallow-sided bird-bath being ideal for the purpose; but whatever is used must allow the bees access to the water without the danger of them falling in and drowning. If possible, screen the hive to prevent it from becoming an eyesore for neighbours, and remember that the bees' flightpath should be as far as possible from places where you or your neighbours are likely to congregate; no one wants squadrons of foraging bees flying across their patios while they are enjoying their garden.

## Protective Clothing

To reduce the chances of being stung and to keep your clothes clean while tending to the hive, either a beesuit or a bee tunic or jacket, available from bee-keeping suppliers, is an essential item. A beesuit is a one-piece unit intended to cover and protect the entire body and which resembles one of the spacesuits worn by astronauts. The drawbacks of beesuits are that they are cumbersome and can be uncomfortable to wear in hot weather. A bee tunic or jacket protects the head, upper body and arms, and should have elasticated sleeves. With this form of clothing, you will, of course, need to make provision for protecting your legs by wearing some loose-fitting, strong trousers that can be tucked snugly into your boots; in this respect, a pair of rubber 'Wellington'-type boots are ideal, but make sure they are wide enough at the tops to take your trousers and provide a gap-free fit when they are tucked inside. Whatever style of clothing you have, it is best to choose a hood

and veil (to protect the head and face) that can be detached by a zipper or similar secure method to prevent bees from getting inside. Most proprietary protective clothing tends to be white, with a darker-coloured mesh or veil for protecting the face. There is a reason for this: in the wild, the bees' natural hive-raiding enemies include bears, skunks and other predators. These tend to be brown or black in colour, so white or light-coloured clothing helps the bees to distinguish the bee-keeper from their usual enemies.

Gloves are an essential item for the beginner, even though they can restrict movement and tend eventually to be discarded by more experienced keepers. Appropriate gloves are available from suppliers, but a pair of strong, close-fitting rubber gloves are a good substitute. Some stores sell strong but supple gloves for general maintenance and DIY, which may also be suitable, but the purpose-made gauntlets, that go some way up the wearer's sleeves, offer the greater protection.

## Smokers

Essential items of equipment as far as the bee-keeper is concerned. There is

OPPOSITE: It is important to wear the correct protective clothing when inspecting the hive.

RIGHT: The smoker is a vital piece of equipment used for controlling the bees.

quite a variation in quality and ease of use in respect of smokers, so try to examine and compare a few different types before making a final choice.

A smoker is a device used to puff smoke into the colony with the purpose of calming the bees so that the hive can be inspected more easily.

It is shaped rather like a coffee pot, and it is essentially a metal can with a spout at the top and a grate at the bottom in which fuel is burned (to make the smoke); there is a simple bellows arrangement attached to it so that the smoke can be forced out of the spout.

So how does the smoke work? The calming effect of smoke on bees has been known since ancient times. First, smoke masks the pheromones that are the bees' chief means of mass communication and which are used by guard or injured bees to alert the hive to potential danger, such as when it is being opened. This breakdown of communication, and thus the chain of command and action, gives the bee-keeper an opportunity to check the hive and close it again without too much disruption to the occupants. The smoke also seems to initiate a feeding response in the bees, presumably because it triggers them to prepare for abandonment of the hive; therefore, they are stoking up on food to be used when the colony first re-establishes itself in a safer place. Also, a fully engorged bee is less likely to sting, so smoke has another positive effect in protecting the bee-keeper.

## Hive Tools

The hive tool is a specially designed piece of equipment that is used as lever, scraper and hook. The tool comes made from wood or stainless steel, and is often brightly coloured since it seems to end up frequently getting lost. It is used when dismantling the hive and when removing frames from it, the scraper part being utilized to remove build-ups of propolis from parts of the hive. Such a range of functions would suggest a complex tool, but in fact the design is quite simple. One of the best types (about 10in /25cm long) resembles an elongated version of the kind of scraper used to remove ice from car windows in winter. One end is flat, broad and sharpened and acts as a scraper, and the other is curved, with a slot near the end, and is used as a lever.

## Hives

The hive is clearly an extremely important item of a bee-keeper's equipment, for it is the place where the honeybees will live and from which honey and other bee products will be harvested. Like so much else in life, beginners can easily be confused by the available choice and may ultimately be seduced by an attractive design, a keen price, or even a supplier's sales patter, and thus buy the wrong type of hive for their purpose. You will soon see that several different types are available, both new and secondhand, some of which are offered ready-assembled, with others coming 'flat-packed' for home assembly. The 'Langstroth' is used almost exclusively in the United States, but also appears in Britain and other parts of the world, while popular hives in Britain are marketed under

LEFT: The hive tool is a universal piece of equipment which every bee-keeper should have.

OPPOSITE: Cross-sections of Langstroth, National and WBC beehives.

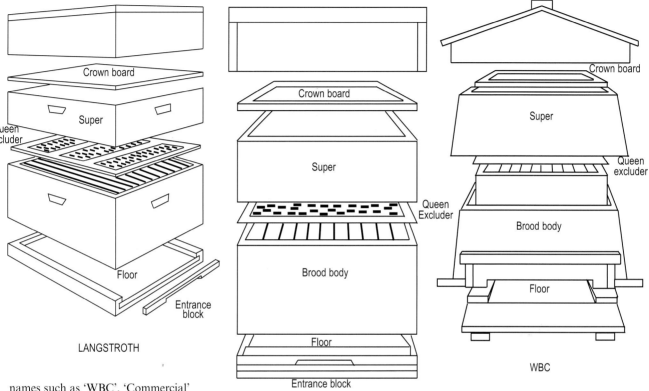

**LANGSTROTH**

Crown board
Super
Queen excluder
Floor
Entrance block

**NATIONAL**

Crown board
Super
Queen Excluder
Brood body
Floor
Entrance block

**WBC**

Crown board
Super
Queen excluder
Brood body
Floor

names such as 'WBC', 'Commercial' and 'National'. The most popular hives are made of wood, though artificial materials, such as polystyrene, are also used. Cedarwood is a popular choice in temperate climates, since it is very durable yet light in weight. Secondhand hives carry the risk of being infected with foulbrood, a disease of honeybees caused by the bacterium *Melissococcus plutonius* or by the more virulent *Paenibacillus larvae*. If there is any doubt concerning the provenance of

such a hive then it is advisable to steer clear of it altogether.

Hives are constructed as a series of boxes, each carrying suspended frames on which the bees build their combs. Above these brood-frame boxes there can normally be fitted a meshlike device known as a queen excluder, the mesh allowing the workers to pass through freely while restricting the

queen because of her larger size. Because she cannot access any frames above the queen excluder, she cannot lay eggs in them, and they are therefore used only for storing the honey. Frames or boxes used for storing honey are called 'supers', and they are obviously of great interest to the honey-collecting bee-keeper. By altering the position of the queen excluder, a bee-keeper can decide how many boxes to allocate to the brood section or to the super section of the hive. (In the active part of the season, when there are plenty of flowers from which to forage, many bee-keepers consider it worth having two supers in use at the same time.)

Each frame consists of a four-sided structure somewhat like a picture frame. Frames may be made of wood or plastic, within which there is either a beeswax-covered plastic foundation sheet, embossed with a honeycomb pattern, or a sheet of honeycomb-embossed pure beeswax set on a wire frame. In either case, the bees build their comb on the foundation sheet. It is advisable not to mix frames in the same box that have been used by bees for brood-rearing and food storage.

At the top of the uppermost box there should be an inner cover. This allows for a gap between the outer top covering of the hive and the hive itself, and helps the airflow as well as preventing heat from the outer cover acting directly on the hive in hot weather. Also, without the inner cover, there is a tendency for the bees to seal the outer cover to the top frame with propolis (a resinous substance), making its removal difficult. Even the inner cover will need to be removed with the flat blade of a hive tool, but this is an easier prospect than levering under the outer cover. To avoid the need to ease the inner cover off, some bee-keepers lay a sheet of canvas over the top frame instead, which can be rolled back when it is necessary to inspect the bees.

Another device is a clearer or an escape board. This is designed to remove the bees from the supers down to the lower boxes and prevent them from returning. This allows the supers to be removed for honey extraction.

The outer cover is a durable waterproof structure at the top of the hive boxes that keeps the weather out. It is usually constructed from wood or plastic. At the base of the hive there is a bottom board with a place for the bees to enter and leave, and usually a platform or ramp that acts as a landing stage and waiting area so that incoming bees can be inspected by the guards. Some bottom boards are fitted with screens to allow debris to fall clear of the hive and to increase the ventilation within.

## Feeders
Feeders are devices that dispense food to bees in the form of sugar syrup. They come in a variety of forms: hive-top feeders are designed to replace the inner cover on the top of the hive, and are made of wood or plastic. They hold up to about 2 gallons (9 litres) of sugar syrup, and can be used at the end of the year to feed the colony.

## Obtaining Bees
There are various means of aquiring bees, some more hazardous than others. The most popular course of action, however, is to obtain stock either from the supplier from which all or some of your equipment came, or from a recognized professional breeder of bees. The bees acquired from one of these sources are much more likely to be good stock, and a reputable breeder shouldn't object to having his bees inspected for disease by an expert before purchase.

Of the different ways to buy bees, first, it is possible to buy a complete colony. This consists of ten or so combs and contains a fertile queen, workers and, depending on the time of year, drones. The whole thing should come complete with stores of food and a brood (developing bees, including eggs, larvae and pupae). Obtaining such a colony in, say, May or June, should make it possible for the colony to produce surplus honey in the first year.

The second method is to buy what is known as a nucleus, which is a small colony consisting of between four and six combs containing a fertile queen, some workers and perhaps some drones. It also includes some food and brood. A nucleus is a much smaller proposition than the complete colony described previously, and will be easier for the beginner to handle. Once installed within the hive the nucleus will, of

A bee-keeper inspecting his Langstroth hives.

course, develop into a complete colony, and may even produce a little honey in the first year.

A third route is to obtain what is called a package. This is a screened or meshed box simply containing honeybees and a queen. Once delivered from the breeder, you must transfer the bees into your own hive and feed them so that they get off to a good start. The other option is to try to obtain a natural swarm of bees, which is a free-living colony without any combs. Early swarms tend to develop well, since they have the whole of the flowering season ahead of them, but late swarms will require plenty of feeding or they will fail to survive the winter.

The other issue regarding swarms is that unless its origin, good health and good temper can be proven, it may turn out to be a bad group of bees that no one would want.

### Transferring Bees to the Hive

Let's assume, first of all, that you have bought a nucleus. The supplier may give instructions on how to transfer the nucleus and the frames to your hive and how to provide any other immediate requirements, such as food for the bees. Before taking delivery of the nucleus, check with the supplier so that you know what to do when it arrives.

The essential procedures are as follows: when the nucleus arrives, place it on the hive stand, open the entrance and allow the bees to fly about for an hour or two. Next, take the nucleus off the hive stand and replace it with the hive. Remove the lid of the nucleus and give a puff or two of smoke from the smoker.

Using your frame tool, prise apart the frames (you may need another puff or two of smoke to keep the bees out of the way as you do this). Lift each frame from the nucleus in turn and place it in the lowermost brood box, keeping the frames in the same sequence. Fill any empty frame spaces with new foundation frames. Put the inner cover on. A feeder with about $1^1/2$ –3 pints (1–2 litres) of sugar syrup should be placed over the feed hole before adding the outer cover. The queen excluder and the first honey super can be installed about a month later, assuming the colony is becoming established in full season.

Alternatively, you may have decided to purchase a package of bees. A typical package weighs about 3lbs (1.4kg) and consists of approximately 3,500 bees. The queen will probably be in a separate queen cage within the package, and the worker bees will be clustered around the cage. Expect to see a few dead bees on the floor of the package box, but if the numbers seem excessive, contact the supplier. If the bees have exhausted their food supply, lightly spray a sugar solution (one-third sugar to two-thirds water in warm water) into the box using a mister. The bees must merely be moistened rather than saturated; don't leave them in the box for any longer than is necessary once they have been delivered, but transfer them to the hive as soon as it is practicable and providing the weather is not too cold. Late afternoon or early evening is a good time to do this.

Before putting the bees into the hive, make sure you have all your equipment to hand, that you are wearing your protective clothing, and that the smoker is lit. You may also need a pair of pliers. Remove the feeder from the package box, then remove the queen

ABOVE LEFT: In spring, the first flowers appear, ready to supplement the hive's dwindling store of food.

OPPOSITE: Children are certain to be fascinated by bees, but must be closely supervised at all times.

cage from the box. Remove any fixings from the feeder, then lift the box and bang it on the ground so that any bees attached to the feeder fall off. Next, remove the queen cage and shake or blow off any bees attached to it. Make sure the queen is alive and looking healthy. At this stage the queen cage can be inserted into the hive by pushing it between the frames in the centre of the lowermost hive box. Ensure that the mesh side faces downwards and that the workers can make contact with the queen. Within the queen cage is a section containing a sugar mixture that must usually be pierced with a pin or small nail.

Now place a second hive box on top of the first one, then remove some of the frames to make a space in which to dump the bees. Get the bees out of the package box by banging the box again, removing the cover and shaking or 'pouring' the bees downwards into the hive. Use the smoker to gently coax them down if necessary. You won't get every single bee out by this method, but when most of them are out, put the package box by the side of the hive so that the rest can come out in their own time, then carefully replace the missing frames from the hive box, trying not to trap any bees as you do so. Now replace the rest of the hive boxes and their frames and the inner and outer covers, attaching a sugar syrup feeder to the hive.

### Inspecting the Hive

Assuming sufficient food has been supplied when first inserting the bees, allow the colony to settle down for three days before inspecting the hive. On opening up the hive, first check the activity of the bees surrounding the queen (don't use smoke before opening the hive because you want to observe the bees' natural reactions). If they seem generally calm, with only a few bees on the cage, it is probably now safe to release the queen. But if her cage is still completely surrounded by bees that are reluctant to be removed, close the hive up and wait for two more days.

When it seems safe to remove the queen, take off the plug covering the queen cage sugar mixture and make sure that the hole is clear by poking it with a pin or small nail. Replace the queen cage between the frames. In a few days the workers will have eaten enough of the sugar mixture for the queen to be released. (Some bee-keepers simply release the queen directly from her cage into the hive during the first inspection, but only if all seems well.) Refill the feeder and close up the hive. A couple of days later, check that the workers have released the queen. If not, release her yourself by opening up her cage and letting her join the other hive members.

### Getting Going

The queen should begin laying about a week after her release. The eggs are tiny white structures resembling miniature grains of sand, and they should be visible within some of the cells built by the worker bees. Discovering eggs is a good sign that all is well and that the colony is beginning to take off and get established. At this stage, keep the feeder topped up, but otherwise leave well alone for about ten days. If, however, no eggs are visible, despite your searches, first make sure that the queen is still present. If she is, it is possible that she wasn't mated before you got her, or that she is in some way unable to lay eggs. When this happens, the only course of action is to replace her with another queen.

As the colony develops and egg-laying proceeds, and as the workers continue to build their comb on the frames of the available boxes, you will need to add a new box of frames as the existing ones get built upon. It may also be necessary to swap around some of

When inspecting the hive, have your smoker at the ready.

the frames in the existing boxes so that they all get used. At this stage, keep using the feeder to supplement the bees' food supply. Make sure you always have sufficient supers ready for when the production of honey begins in earnest. The best advice is always to be aware of what is happening inside the hive with regard to brood, comb-production and honey storage, adjusting the number of frames you provide accordingly. External conditions should also be taken into account: for example, what is the weather like? Is it conducive to bee activity? Are there plenty of local blooms available?

# A PRACTICAL GUIDE TO SELF-SUFFICIENCY

## Inspecting the Established Colony

There is often much to do when the hive is opened and, especially for the novice confronted by bees upset by the invasion of their home, it can be difficult to remember why you are inspecting the hive in the first place. Try to memorize the following before opening up:

• Does everything seem normal? Are the bees fairly active? Is there evidence of disease present? (Admittedly, such questions may only be answered adequately with experience.)
• Does the colony have enough food?
• Is all the space being filled? Is another super needed?
• Is the queen laying eggs? Is there older brood as well as eggs?
• Can you see new queen cells? Is the colony going to swarm?

## Harvesting Honey

Numerous books and websites are devoted to the subject of harvesting, extracting and putting honey into jars, but below is a general account of the process, which describes the main stages and the options available. Honey extraction is a somewhat messy business requiring a few pieces of specialized equipment, some method of temperature regulation, and a little know-how. Should you decide this aspect of bee-keeping is not for you, other bee-keepers may be willing to perform the task for you.

You will know when it is time to begin collecting the honey because the supers will have their honeycombs closed off with wax coverings. Get your smoker lit, put on your protective clothing and have your hive tool to hand. The first job is to get all the bees out of the super, or supers, from which the honey is to be obtained. To facilitate this, a bee escape is used. This is a board that is placed under the super you wish to remove. It contains an exit that allows the bees to move down into the brood area, but prevents them from returning to the honey super. Give the bees 24 hours to vacate the super. Some bee-keepers use a fume board to encourage them to leave; this is a special board with a cloth impregnated with a safe chemical, such as benzaldehyde or butric anhydride, the first of which smells like bitter almonds and which can be obtained from bee-keeping suppliers. When a fume board is used, it normally takes only a quarter of an hour or so for the bees to leave; the chemical is not poisonous to them, they merely find it offensive. Another method is to use a mechanical blower to forcibly remove the bees from the super, having first removed it from the hive. The super should be placed on top of the hive with the bottom of it facing the back of the hive before a blast is directed through the frames. In any case, a light smoking is useful to begin the evacuation process.

## Extracting and Bottling Honey

Once the bees have vacated the box, the frames containing the honey can be removed. Honey extraction should be carried out in a clean room using clean materials; the honey will flow better if the temperature is warm. In many ways a kitchen is the ideal place, being warm and with access to power and running water. This may not accord with everyone's idea of what a kitchen should be used for, however, and so a utility room or even a garage may have to double up as an extraction room, provided it is not adjacent to a lavatory. Hands must be thoroughly clean, with waterproof dressings covering cuts, and clean protective clothing must be worn. Clean up as you go along.

All equipment must be of food-grade plastic or stainless steel. First get a bucket and place some cheese cloth inside it, allowing some of the material to drape over the edges. Now place a piece of wood approximately 3 x 2in (7.5 x 5cm) thick across the top of the bucket. A couple of notches cut out to make it fit the rim of the bucket without slipping around, and another on the opposite side to hold the frame securely, will greatly assist the task that follows. Now, resting one end of the frame on the piece of wood, cut or carve off the wax cappings that seal the comb, leaning the frame slightly at an angle so that the cappings fall off without sticking back onto the frame lower down. A proprietary uncapping knife (some are heated to make the task easier) or a sharp, strong carving knife are suitable for the purpose, using the two edges of the frame as cutting guides. You will see the capping fall into the bucket. The honey that flows out with the cappings can be gathered once it has drained through the cloth. Once you have completed one side, turn the frame over and do the same with the other side. Once the process is understood, more efficient ways of collecting and straining the honey may be devised – perhaps a plastic box with a fine filter can be used, set above a second box with a tap built into the side near the bottom to allow the collected honey to flow out.

The honeycomb should now be placed in an extractor, of which there are several types, chief among them being the radial and the tangential, named according to the way the frames are held in the unit. Both, however, extract the honey by using centrifugal force – rather like the action of a spin-drier removing water. The best extractors are made from food-grade polythene or stainless steel; other materials are not suitable for honey that is intended for public consumption. Some extractors are driven by electric motors and others are operated by turning a handle. It is also possible to hire a good extractor from bee-keeping associations rather than

buying one. Always follow the manufacturer's instructions, paying attention to the way the extractor is loaded and cleaned after use.

The honey should then be finely strained directly from the extractor, a task made easier if it is warm, bearing in mind that once the honey starts to granulate it will not pass through a sieve unless it is warmed. The strained honey is collected in a bucket prior to bottling. The best way to remove honey

from the bucket is by means of a tap, called a honey gate, and it is an easy task to fit one yourself, nylon honey gates, with the necessary washers and fixings, being readily available. Cut a hole near to the bottom of a plastic bucket and fit on the honey gate. Again, you will need to warm the honey so that it flows easily out of the bucket and into jars. If you are competent at DIY, a simple way to do this is to build a warming box comprising a couple of electric light bulbs (each about 40W). Place the buckets on the warming box until the honey is of the desired consistency but without overheating it.

Jars must be perfectly clean and dry and preferably sterilized by filling each clean jar with water and microwaving it on full power for five minutes, depending on the size (make sure there are no metal parts on the jar). Empty, and allow to cool. Low, wide-necked jars are preferable so that the honey can be more easily removed. Once the honey has been poured into the jars they should be carefully sealed to prevent moisture absorption, which may cause fermentation, then labelled and dated. Attractive labels may be purchased for a more professional look.

Unless you produce honey on an industrial scale, using bees that have been restricted to specific flowers (such as heather), it is unlikely you will be able to identify the type of flower from which it came, for during the course of a season the bees will have collected nectar and pollen from all manner of flowering plants. This will be very evident once the honey extraction

process is begun; the colour of the honey may vary considerably, reflecting the shades and colours of the flower products from which it originated.

Having such a high sugar content, and being a natural antibacterial and antifungal, honey is considered a low-risk food. The above method is primarily intended for use at home when preparing honey for your own personal use. Some bee-keepers sell honey only occasionally in small and variable amounts according to the size of the harvest and the honey that is surplus to their requirements each year. Others, with a greater number of hives, may regard their bee-keeping as a sideline to earn extra money and may be supplying various retail outlets on a regular basis.

Remember that the rules are rather more stringent for bee-keepers supplying honey for sale to the public. In the United States, the Federal Food

OPPOSITE: Honeycomb before the honey has been extracted.

RIGHT: The honey can be poured into sterilized jars once it has been strained.

and Drug Administration or US Department of Agriculture should first be approached, while in England HM Government's requirements covering production, labelling and lot numbering should be consulted (see internet). (Other parts of Britain have their own statutory requirements.) Statutory regulations change from time to time, and your local Environmental Health Officer should also be approached for advice. Advisory leaflet No. 103: *So You Wish To Sell Honey*, also attempts to set out and clarify these requirements, and may be obtained from: BBKA The Bee Centre, National Agricultural Centre, Stoneleigh, Warwickshire, CV8.

## Uses of Honey

This may seem an obvious and unnecessary section to include. After all, honey is for eating isn't it? Well, yes, of course it is, but honey has more to offer than simply being a form of food. Historically, it has been used as a trading commodity, as a natural preservative and as the basis for the alcoholic drink known as mead, but honey also plays a large role in medicine. For 2,700 years, and maybe even longer, humans have used honey to treat all manner of ailments, applying it to wounds, for example, to combat infection and speed the healing process, although it is only fairly recently that the antiseptic and

antibacterial properties of honey have been fully explored. Honey is now approved as an agent to help combat the dangerous MRSA bacteria, and it is also used in the treatment of diabetic ulcers. The antioxidants present in honey have also been attributed to the alleviation of conditions such as colitis, which is an inflammation of the colon.

Patients, after their tonsils have been removed, are often prescribed honey, and indeed honey has been used for centuries to relieve sore throats and coughs, either taken in liquid form or in the form of honey lozenges. A particularly effective remedy to ease sore throats and relieve the affects of colds and flu can be achieved by sipping a mixture of two teaspoonfuls of honey with the juice of half a lemon from a cup topped up with hot water. Adults may find this drink even more beneficial if a small tot of whisky is also added, especially at bedtime!

Cookery books are packed with recipes using honey; indeed, many of them are devoted solely to the art of cooking with this ingredient. Honey adds sweetness, body, a unique flavour and a delicious glaze to many dishes, and goes especially well with meats such as pork (and ham), chicken and duck, as well as with fish such as salmon. Food can be coated with honey, or it can be one of the ingredients of a marinade or sauce for meat or vegetables. It is often used to

top waffles, fruit salads, breakfast cereals and yogurts, or as a spread on bread or toast.

Apart from its use in making mead, of which there are numerous varieties, honey can be used in several other types of drinks, including spicy mulled wines.

## Other Bee Products

Another useful commodity extracted from bees is the substance known as royal jelly, which is a secretion produced by the hypopharyngeal glands of worker bees and fed to developing larvae. Royal jelly is produced commercially by stimulating the colony to produce queen bees, from which the royal jelly is collected when the larvae are only a few days old. It is practical only to collect the royal jelly from developing queens, for although other larvae are also fed the substance for a few days, only queens receive a store of it that can be collected. During the processing of royal jelly, honey and beeswax are also added to help in its preservation.

Royal jelly is sold as a dietary supplement, and it is claimed to have various health benefits, due mainly to its high vitamin content, especially the B-complex. Royal jelly may also have some value in boosting the immune system, in the stimulation of stem cells in the brain, in lowering cholesterol, and as an antibiotic and anti-inflammatory – properties that are unlikely to be fulfilled if the product is ingested, when they are neutralized. Royal jelly is also a component of some beauty products.

Beeswax is another natural product, secreted from special glands on the abdomens of worker bees. The wax is used for building the comb cells in which the young are raised and the pollen and honey stored. Beeswax is also variously used around hives to fill in gaps. During the honey extraction process, the wax cappings are cut from the comb. The colour of the wax varies according to the types of flowers on which the bees were feeding, but it is generally yellow, although it can vary from nearly white to brown. The wax is sieved off and gathered during the honey extraction process to be purified before being put to a variety of uses. As well as the many historical uses of beeswax, which included the making of candles, seals and sculptures, clarified beeswax is still used for candle-making today, as a lubricant in the woodworking and cabinet-making trade, for the smooth operation of drawers and windows, and in wood and shoe polishes when dissolved in turpentine.

Beeswax is occasionally used as a coating for cheeses and in the cosmetics industry (for example, as hair pomade), and is used in medicine to make dentistry casts and barrier creams, the

cosmetics and pharmaceutical industries accounting for more than 50 per cent of the total consumption. It is quite possible for bee-keepers to collect and refine beeswax for use in some of the aforementioned, and there are many books and websites that explain in detail exactly how this may be achieved.

Honey and its by-products have proven their worth over the centuries.

CHAPTER SIX

# WILD FOODS

*E*dible wild plants are free, delicious and nutritious and it is great fun to look for them when out for a walk.

An interest in the food plants that grow wild in the countryside, and along the seashore, increases the enjoyment of a ramble through woods and fields and along hedgerows and water margins. Whether on a solitary walk, or on a family outing, develop the habit of looking out for what our ancestors regarded as valuable foods, which have never been developed and cultivated yet add a pleasurable dimension to the rural scene. Here, some of the commoner wild food plants are discussed which, gathered in small amounts at a time, will not deplete their habitat but can be regarded as occasional and welcome additions to everyday meals. Remember also that there are rules to follow when gathering free food from wild sources.

Most important is to be able to identify anything you are going to eat. Since this can only be a general guide, check any plants you do not recognize against a specialist botanical reference book before even attempting to remove them, let alone eat them. Some plants, such as members of the umbellifer family, can be very similar to one another and some are poisonous while others are not. Certainly if you are aiming to gather wild mushrooms you will need the guidance of an expert on the subject as well as a very comprehensive and well-illustrated guide before venturing to pick and eat.

Every so often there are reports of a tragic death when someone has eaten a death cap or other lethal fungus, having mistaken it for one that is harmless. It is advisable, therefore, to familiarize yourself with and limit yourself to what can be regarded as the five 'foolproof' mushrooms – chicken of the woods (also known as sulphur bracket fungus found on oak trees), giant puffball, morel, chanterelle and porcini (ceps) – but be very aware that it is still possible to confuse some of these with other similar but very poisonous species.

### Where to Find Edible Plants
Keep your eyes open and you will begin

OPPOSITE: Wild strawberries are small but very delicious.

RIGHT: Elderflowers can be used to make cordials, while the berries that come after can be transformed into a robust red wine.

uncultivated areas, making them places to be avoided at all costs. Remember that the same applies to streams and ditches, where water may be polluted with weedkillers and insecticides washed off from the land.

Good places to look are along unfrequented country lanes, disused railroad tracks, on downs, moors, hills and in woods, forests, by river banks and in marshland and shoreline.

Certain plants are protected species, while others are becoming rarer as time goes on, the cowslip, once so widely used in country wines, being one such an example. The plants mentioned here

to notice the places where certain plants grow and thrive, although there are many locations to avoid, such as the verges of busy highways exposed to car exhaust fumes. Also hazardous are the chemical sprays used on cultivated crops, which may blow onto

OPPOSITE: In various parts of the United States, wild blackberries are known as 'black-caps', a term more commonly used for black raspberries (*Rubus occidentalis*).

ABOVE: Bullaces are wild members of the plum family and make excellent jelly/jam.

RIGHT: Hedge garlic (*Alliara petiola*) is one of the earliest of the hedgerow plants, its bright green leaves appearing in February.

are common ones, but once your interest in the subject expands, you may wish to extend your knowledge. If in doubt, check with a local or national conservation society or in a good reference book on the subject.

Resist the urge to pick too many plants at a time; in fact, if there are only a few specimens, it is better to leave them alone to spread and colonize for another year. Make sure to gather a few leaves or berries from a number of plants, rather than stripping a particular plant completely bare. There are, of course, some plants that are very prolific to which such caution does not apply, such as nettles, fat hen, dandelions and blackberries, which can be used in a number of different ways, while the rarer 'finds' can add an unusual, even decorative touch, to just one or two other dishes.

Use a lightweight polythene bowl, other than bags, when blackberrying or collecting other soft fruits. This will protect the fruit and keep it in good condition until you get it home.

OPPOSITE: Watercress (*Nasturtium officinale*), a member of the mustard family, is naturalized in springs and wet ground in temperate climates. It is considered to be one of the super foods, being especially rich in iron.

LEFT: Some species of seaweed are edible and rich in minerals and vitamins.

BELOW: Collect dandelion leaves for a tasty salad in early spring, preferably before the flowers appear.

Keep a notebook, which you can refer back to from time to time. In it you can record when and what you picked and where, and even how you used the various plants in particular recipes.

## What and When to Pick

Most plants are at their best for eating when the leaves are young. Choose leaves undamaged by insects or disease. Fruit must be ripe, but not past its best, and nuts must fill their shells and not be too green. It is best to pick in the morning when the dew has disappeared but before the 'crop' has become exposed to too much sun. Avoid damaging hedgerows and other plants as you carefully pick the ones you want. All wild food is better eaten as soon as possible after picking, so it pays to note the spot where the plants you like are growing, and collect them just before you are ready to eat them.

## What Not to Pick

Keep a list by you of strictly non-edible plants, adding to it as your knowledge grows. The list below will start you off, but it is by no means comprehensive.

These plants should **NOT** be eaten:

*Aconitum anglicum* (monkshood)
*Arum maculatum* (cuckoo pint)
*Atropa belladonna* (deadly nightshade)
*Bryonia dioica* (white bryony)
*Colchicum autumnale* (autumn crocus)
*Conium maculatum* (hemlock)
*Convallaria majalis* (lily of the valley)
*Digitalis purpurea* (foxglove)
*Euonymus europaeus* (spindle tree)
*Hedera helix* (ivy)
*Helleborus viridis* (green hellebore)
*Hyoscyamus niger* (henbane)
*Ilex aquifolium* (holly)
*Mercurialis perennis* (dog's mercury)
*Oenanthe crocata* (hemlock water dropwort)
*Ranunculus* (all buttercups)
*Taxus baccata* (yew)
*Viscum album* (mistletoe)

LEFT: Alexanders: the stems can be cooked like asparagus and eaten with melted butter.

OPPOSITE ABOVE: Nettles should be handled with care, but they are good in soups.

OPPOSITE BELOW: St. Georges mushrooms are a sublime taste of spring, but make sure you know what you are picking.

plants as chickweed, young dandelion leaves, primroses, daisies and watercress will all add interest as well as minerals and vitamins to a run-of-the-mill dish.

Many plants taste like spinach when cooked, one of the best being fat hen, which is a very ancient food plant indeed. This can be found growing in ploughed fields, dug-over gardens and even on construction sites. Young nettles, too, made into soup, are an obvious choice, but they can be used in a number of other interesting ways and so too can dead nettles, both red and white.

Ground elder, abhorred by gardeners as a pernicious weed, is another candidate for the cooking pot, having a unique flavour all its own, while the stems of some plants also

Fungi have not been listed here as picking them should be avoided altogether unless you are expert at recognizing them (see page 187).

## Using Wild Foods

Our country ancestors must have enjoyed a varied diet throughout the year, for even in winter there are still a few leaves and berries to be found. Use leaves and flowers raw in salads, sprinkled with chopped herbs and with a good dressing of oil and vinegar or lemon juice. Try an all-wild mix in spring, or add wild plants to a lettuce and cucumber salad. Such modest

LEFT: Sweet chestnuts are delicious roasted, but they can also be made into a tasty stuffing for game birds and poultry.

BELOW: Sloes are the fruit of the blackthorn, and although naturally sour, they can be added with sugar to gin to give it a wonderful flavour.

OPPOSITE: Beautiful and colourful wild woodland berries

areas, the beautiful feathery wild fennel. Flavourings from such plants as Jack-by-the hedge and ramsons taste mildly but unmistakably of garlic, and tansy or alexanders seeds, used in moderation, also make good eating.

make delicious eating. Alexanders stems, cooked like asparagus and eaten with melted butter, make a memorable feast, or they can be candied like angelica to enjoy as a sweet treat or cake decoration. Hogweed stems, unlikely as it may seem, are also good, both on their own or stir-fried with other vegetables, and so are burdock stems, provided they are picked young.

Roots are also usable, the most obvious examples being in horseradish sauce and dandelion coffee.

Look out for wild herbs in particular. There are a number of mints, all delicious, and you may be lucky enough to find wild thyme, marjoram and, especially in coastal

Berries and fruits are always worth seeking out, wild strawberries being among the most delectable, but sloes, bullaces, rowanberries, crab apples, rosehips, haws and blackberries are not to be despised and can be the basis of many delicious jams and jellies. You may be fortunate enough to live in an area where bilberries, with their unforgettable, rich flavour, grow wild, or stumble across a few cranberries, though these are not commonly found in the wild.

Edible fungi, already mentioned, are some of the most highly prized of the wild foods, especially truffles, which grow below ground and must be sought out by specially trained dogs. These command especially high prices, particularly from restaurant chefs. Seaweeds, too, repay trial and experiment, both to eat and to use in health-giving baths. Late in the season, go looking for nuts, which can be used in many dishes, or simply enjoyed raw. On page 214, you will find a chapter on preserving wild foods in a variety of ways, from drying to bottling, and from concocting ketchups and cordials to wine-making.

Hopefully these ideas will transform the mundane task of preparing meals into a rewarding and fascinating hobby, especially when you think of all the free nourishment you are gaining from plants which have been grown without the dubious benefit

of artificial fertilizers and which have not been polluted by chemical sprays or insecticides.

The history of the plants themselves repays some research, for many of them have been used for hundreds of years, either for food or medicinally, and often they have interesting connections with magic or as protection against the fairies or little people. Their country names can be charming and amusing; fat hen was once known as 'muck weed', in that it often grew on manure heaps; 'bumblekite' was a country name for blackberries and, because of its known properties as a diruretic, the dandelion is also known as 'pissabed'!

# CHAPTER SEVEN

# SELF-SUFFICIENCY IN THE HOME

## HOW TO REDUCE YOUR ENERGY CONSUMPTION

*Tips for saving electricity and cutting energy costs. Remember to get the whole family involved and you will save an appreciable amount of money.*

### 1. Unplug

Unplug seldom-used appliances, such as that extra refrigerator in the basement that is only used occasionally. Remember that keeping only a few items in a fridge is wasteful as fridges run more economically when kept full.

Every house is full of little electric chargers, used to replenish cell phones, PDAs, digital cameras, cordless tools and other personal gadgets. Keep them unplugged until you need them.

Use power strips to switch off televisions, home theatre equipment and stereos when you're not using them. Even when you think these products are switched off, their 'standby' consumption can be equivalent to a 75 or 100W light bulb left on continuously.

Unplug anything you are not using and don't leave appliances on standby.

## 2. Set Computers to Sleep and Hibernate

Activate the 'sleep mode' feature on your computer so that it will use less power during periods of inactivity.

The power management settings in Microsoft PCs are to be found on the control panel, while Mac users should look for the energy-saving settings under system preferences in the Apple menu.

Set your computer to 'hibernate' automatically after 30 minutes or so of inactivity. The mode turns the computer off in a way that doesn't

require you to reload everything when you switch it back on, and is more energy- and time-efficient than shutting down and restarting your computer from scratch.

## 3. Take Control of Temperature

If you want your home to be comfortably warm when you wake up in the morning or come in from an outing, then the timer/programmer should be used to switch the heating on beforehand. You can time how quickly your home heats up and cools down by switching the boiler on and measuring

ABOVE: Set your thermostat to a comfortable temperature and to 'off' when not at home.

LEFT: Use the energy-saving sleep mode on your computer during short periods of inactivity.

the time taken to reach a comfortable temperature. If this is, for example, 30 minutes, then set the programmer to switch the heating on 30 minutes in advance. Leaving the heating on for any longer than this when you are out of the house, even on a low setting, means that the boiler will be working continuously when the heating is not needed, and all the energy it produces will be wasted.

Set the thermostat on your water heater between 120°F (48°C) and 130°F (54°C). This may seem too cool for some, but by keeping temperatures as low as possible energy will be saved. But although using lower temperatures saves energy, however, you might end up using extra electricity to boost the water temperature in your dishwasher.

Burning wood is considered carbon-neutral and cost-effective and a good way of using up fallen trees and branches. A wood-burning stove may also heat your water.

Close shades and blinds during the summer or when the air conditioner is in use or will be in use later in the day.

## 4. Use Appliances Efficiently

Set the temperature of a refrigerator at 38–42°F (3°C to 5°C), and a freezer at between 0°C and 5°F (-17 to -15°C). Use the power-save switch if your fridge has one, and make sure the door seals fit tightly. You can check this by making sure a bank note, closed in between the door gaskets, is difficult to pull out. If

OPPOSITE: Never overload the dryer with heavy items such as towels.

ABOVE: Hang washing outside to dry whenever possible. Not only does it cost nothing but your laundry will also smell that much fresher.

it slides easily between the gaskets, then they should be replaced.

Don't preheat or 'peek' inside the oven more than is necessary. Check the seal on the oven door, and use a microwave oven for cooking or reheating small items.

Wash only full loads in your dishwasher, using short cycles for all but the dirtiest dishes. This saves water and the energy used to pump and heat it. Air-drying crockery can also reduce energy use.

In your clothes washer, set the appropriate water level for the size of the load; wash in cold water when practical, and always rinse in cold. Clean the lint filter in the dryer after every use.

Dry heavy and light fabrics separately and don't add wet items to a load that's already partly dry. If available, use the moisture sensor setting. Remember that an outdoor clothes line is the most energy-efficient clothes dryer of all!

### 5. Turn Out the Lights

Don't forget to flick the light switch when you leave a room, which also applies to the office, too. Turn out or dim the lights in unused conference rooms, and when you decide to step out for lunch.

Work by daylight, when possible. A typical commercial building uses more energy for lighting than anything else.

### Buildings and Insulation

Around half of all your expensive heat can escape if your home is not properly insulated, so instead of turning up the thermostat, see about getting this done. By following the guidelines below you will substantially save on energy bills and make a massive reduction in your carbon footprint into the bargain.

1. Stop energy loss via the doors. Fit draft-excluders around all exterior doors, and interior if necessary. Sealant strips can be bought cheaply from DIY stores and are very easy to fit (just like applying sticky tape). Don't forget to get a brush trim for letter boxes, larger gaps and the bottom of doors.

LEFT: Replace light bulbs with energy-saving ones wherever possible. This can make quite a saving to your energy bill in the course of a year and they last much longer into the bargain.

OPPOSITE: Heat rises and is lost through the roof, so be sure to insulate the loft space.

2. Make sure windows are well-insulated. Cracks and crevices around window frames are a typical escape route for warm air. To check your windows, run the palm of your hand around the edge of the frame. If you feel a breeze, then cold air is coming in. Patch the weak points up using putty or another filler.

3. It is well-worth investing in double glazing if you don't already have it. Check first, however, that your local planning regulations permit it as some older or historic buildings may have preservation orders on them.

4. Use heavy window dressings to assist insulation. Closing curtains or blinds after dark also traps in the warm air and prevents drafts. Ideally use curtains and blinds with thermal backings for added heat retention.

5. Fill in any floor gaps. Most homes have gaps between skirting boards and floors, and there is likely to be quite a few between older, stripped floorboards, too, for which a silicone sealer can be used.

If you are thinking about having a new wooden floor laid, it would be a good idea to get experts in to fit floor insulation before the boards are laid down. An alternative would be to have fitted carpets with a good-quality underlay.

6. Insulating the loft or roof space in the average home is likely to save a huge amount of energy, resulting in a major reduction in fuel bills. This is one of the most efficient, cheap and simple energy-saving options, and anyone can do it for themselves.

7. If there is a 'cold wall' in your home, usually constructed from concrete or brick, which has little or no insulation, it is possible to fit a 4–6in (10–15cm) plasterboard to it. The process is very

simple, effective and above all cheap. A plasterer will fit this for you and finish off the joins with a coat of wet plaster. Not only will this add valuable insulation to your home, but the wall will also appear considerably warmer to the touch and reduce condensation.

8. Wrap your hot water tank in a cosy 3.5-in (80-mm) jacket. This will not only cut heat loss by 75 per cent, but you will also recoup the cost of buying the jacket in fewer than 6 months.

## SOLAR POWER

*Using solar power to heat and power the home, as well as industry, is still a relatively new concept. Solar energy is free, it needs no fuel and it produces no waste or pollution. Because the sun will hopefully keep on shining, it is also a renewable source of energy, so it makes sense to use it.*

### Advantages of Solar Power

For some time now, doing something for the environment has been an important issue. Solar power creates no pollution and there are no carbon emissions, so its use may well be an ultimate solution to the problem of climate change. Sunlight is free and available all over the planet. It will never run out and it is a completely renewable resource.

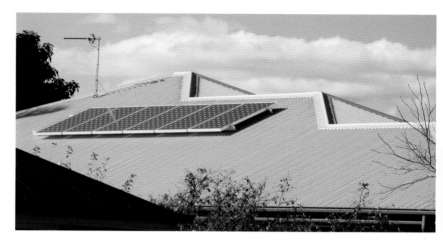

Because of the many problems our planet is currently facing, an alternative source of energy is urgently needed. Currently, fossil fuels are widely used to generate electricity, but with the burning of such fuels, global warming will continue to become that much more pronounced. Understandably, many of us are becoming increasingly concerned and are already opting for solar-powered homes. Moreover, you don't need to be rich to make the switch since the systems available these days have become that much more affordable.

Once the initial cost of installing a solar power system has been found, the benefits will also go a long way towards fulfilling the quest for self-sufficiency.

### What is Solar Power?

Solar power is the conversion of sunlight into electricity, either directly using photovoltaics (PV), or indirectly using concentrated solar power (CSP), or to split water and create hydrogen fuel using techniques of artificial photosynthesis. Concentrated solar power systems use lenses or mirrors and tracking systems to focus a large area of sunlight into a small beam. Photovoltaics converts light into electric current using the photoelectric effect.

Today, solar-powered devices such as flashlights, pool purifiers, ventilators, mosquito inhibitors, heaters, fountain

ABOVE: Solar roof panels.

FAR LEFT: Solar-powered lights for the garden are easy to install and cost nothing to run.

OPPOSITE: A solar hot water system.

pumps, radios, lighting, and many more are readily available. Even though the initial cost of buying such devices may be substantial, think of them as one-time investments that will pay for themselves in the long run.

## Solar Panels

Solar panels use light energy (photons) from the sun to generate electricity through the photovoltaic effect. The structural (load-carrying) member of a module can either be the top layer or the back layer. The majority of modules use wafer-based crystalline silicon cells or thin-film cells based on cadmium telluride or silicon. The conducting wires that take the current off the panels may contain silver, copper or other conductive (but generally not magnetic) transition metals.

If you are thinking of installing solar panels on your house, remember that because they produce energy from sunlight and thin cloud, energy will not be produced all the time, so don't disconnect yourself from the main power supply as you will need it to cut in on rainy days. Likewise, if you live in the northern hemisphere, where there are short, dark days for much of the winter, solar power may not be a worthwile proposition, although it may well be an attractive option in places where days are long and sunny.

Solar energy systems tend to pay for themselves over time (average time for payback is four years), and it may even be possible to make money out of your system by selling surplus power back to the main energy supplier. Some manufacturers may install solar panels at a reduced cost but will retain any profits made from the surplus energy.

The good news is that solar energy systems are robust, silent and very reliable. They are also useful in remote places where mains electricity is not an option. Silicon, moreover, which is used for semi-conductors, is the second most abundant mineral on Earth.

## WIND POWER

*Mankind has been harnessing the wind in one way or another for thousands of years. Today it has another use, that of generating electricity.*

### Advantages of Wind Power

A Wind Energy Converter, or wind generator, is a device that converts the potential energy in the wind to another form of wind power energy, which can either be mechanical or electrical. When the wind blows, the rotor blade stops a percentage of the wind, and that percentage is converted into energy. According to physics, the maximum amount of wind energy that can be converted is 59.3 per cent. This is known as the Betz Limit.

There are a number of types of wind generators and research has been done on virtually every possible concept with the objective of producing the maximum amount of power for the lowest cost with the highest possible reliability. Experiments have found the horizontal axis upwind or downwind design to be the best concept. The most common designs include:

• Horizontal Upwind – The generator shaft is positioned horizontally and the wind hits the blade before the tower.
• Horizontal Downwind – The generator shaft is positioned horizontally and the wind hits the tower first then the blade.

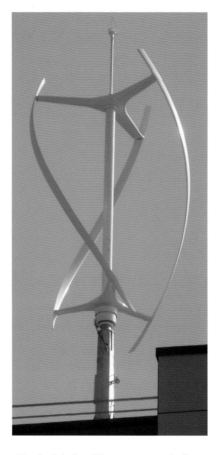

• Vertical Axis – The generator shaft is positioned vertically with the blades pointing up with the generator mounted on the ground or on a short tower.

If there is the option of using renewable energy in your home, then you may be considering a domestic wind turbine, which, in essence, is a much smaller version of the turbines which now dot the landscape. A domestic wind turbine can be fitted to your house or in a suitable location very close to the building, and the energy derived from it will go towards powering your home.

In order to fully power a modern home, the domestic wind turbine would need to span 16ft (5m) from tip to tip on a predominantly windy site. The average household consumption is approximately 4500kW hours and a domestic wind turbine with a span of 2m might yield 500kW hours per year in favourable conditions. The energy produced by the turbine can be used to charge batteries or be connected to your national electricity supplier. In many cases, home-owners use a domestic wind turbine to supplement the energy they receive from their national supplier, thus reducing their bills but not being entirely reliant on the wind.

Individual turbines vary in size and power output from a few hundred watts to two or three megawatts (as a guide, a typical domestic system would be 2.5–6kW, depending on the location and size of the home). Small domestic systems are relatively inexpensive to buy and have installed, although these small turbines may not contribute significantly to your energy needs. Please check with your local authority

OPPOSITE: A vertical axis wind generator.

RIGHT: Most countries require planning permission before a wind generator is installed.

BELOW: Double energy: a small wind generator and solar panel combined.

before installing a wind turbine as permission is often required.

Wind power is proportional to the cube of the wind's speed, so relatively minor increases in speed result in large changes in potential output.

## DOMESTIC HYDROPOWER

*Although renewable energy is a hot topic at the moment, few know much about hydropower, and this is especially true when applied to the home.*

People think it is a fairly new technology, when renewable sources of electricity are mentioned, but hydropower is without doubt one of the oldest forms of producing such energy in existence. Waterwheels, the first form of hydropower, were used for irrigation in the Far East over 2,000 years ago, while they have also long been utilized in milling grain.

If there is naturally falling water near your home then it will also be possible to harness the energy by using a domestic hydropower system. These are very small systems which can be used without damaging the environment. Large-scale hydropower schemes have been seen to be damaging, but these small-scale plants do not cause as much disturbance. As long as they are managed correctly they shouldn't create any environmental problems.

There are several different types of turbines which can be used depending on the project in question. In each case the turbine spins a shaft which is used to generate electricity. There are two main categories of turbine.

• Impulse turbines are where pressurized jets hit shaped cups. This means that virtually all of the water's energy can be captured.

• Reaction turbines, on the other hand, are where the water is not pressurized into a jet and the water simply passes over the blades. This causes the blades to spin, and so creates movement which can be converted into electricity.

Before you consider installing hydropower systems you must check with your local authority whether or not you need to apply for permission before initiating such a scheme.

By using small-scale systems there are actually environmental benefits: for a start the need to use fossil fuels and other methods of energy production is reduced. Micro-hydropower systems can also provide power for properties located in isolated areas where there are no other options when it comes to installing electricity.

Hydroelectric production accounts for 20 per cent of the world's electrical supply. Such power stations are popular in Norway, which produces most of its electricity from this method. Iceland and Austria also produce in excess of 70 per cent of their electricity through hydropower plants.

**There are three different types of hydroelectric system:-**

• **Diversion** This is where a portion of a river is diverted through a man-made canal; this can be done without using a dam and is consequently not as damaging to the environment.

• **Impoundment** This is the most popular for large-scale systems, in which a dam is constructed across a river which creates a lake behind it. The result is a body of water which can be used to drive a turbine to create electricity.

• **Pumped Storage** Water can be pumped from a lower reservoir to a higher reservoir if only a small amount of electricity is required. When more is required the water can be used to turn a turbine and so create electricity. In other words, the water is being used to store the energy, rather like a battery.

Domestic hydropower projects are encouraged by the Low Carbon Buildings programme and therefore may be eligible for grants depending on the country in which you live.

### Suitable Conditions for Micro-Hydropower

The best geographical sites for exploiting small-scale hydropower are those where there are rivers, passing through great mountain ranges and their foothills, that flow all year round,

This traditional style of waterwheel is used to produce energy.

accompanied by high year-round rainfall. Low-head turbines have been developed for small-scale exploitation of rivers or irrigation canals where there is a small head but sufficient flow to provide adequate power.

To assess the suitability of a potential site, the hydrology of the site needs to be assessed and a site survey carried out to determine actual flow and head data. Hydrological information can be obtained from the meteorology or irrigation department, usually run by the national government. This data gives a good overall picture of annual rain patterns and likely fluctuations in precipitation and, therefore, flow patterns.

The site survey gives more detailed information of the site conditions to allow power calculation to be made and design work to begin. Flow data should be gathered over a period of at least one full year, where possible, so as to ascertain the fluctuation in river flow over the various seasons. There are many methods for carrying out flow and head measurements and these can be found in relevant texts or by consulting on-line resources.

## Turbines

A turbine converts the energy in falling water into shaft power. There are various types of turbine which can be categorized in one of several ways. The choice of turbine will depend mainly on the pressure head available and the design flow for the proposed hydropower installation. If you are considering the installation of a hydropower system, consult an expert in the field before proceeding further.

## TREATING SEWAGE

*Mains sewage systems, while effective, use millions of gallons/litres of water each year and also pump millions of tons of carbon dioxide into the atmosphere. There are simple ways to save water and the environment, such as by not flushing every time, or by installing a more water-efficient toilet. But best of all, if circumstances permit, is to use one of the systems described below.*

## COMPOST TOILETS

A compost toilet is dry or waterless, i.e. one that doesn't use water to take the waste somewhere else; it also allows natural processes to produce useful compost after a resting period depending on the type of toilet. There are usually two chambers – one in use and one resting. A typical toilet would use one chamber for a year, then change to the second chamber and allow the first to decompose for a year before emptying.

Such toilets don't smell, as long as there is a vent pipe and a drain to take away excess liquid. A handful of a soak (straw or sawdust etc.) is dropped into the toilet after each use. This is because bacteria like to feed on a balanced diet of carbon and nitrogen, and as human waste contains a lot of nitrogen, if they don't get enough carboniferous material (like sawdust, straw, hay, shredded paper) they will give off excess nitrogen in the form of ammonia, which accounts for the smell. The soak also allows oxygen into the pile and absorbs liquid. This allows the pile to decompose aerobically to produce nitrates, phosphates and sulphates. Without a soak, the pile will decompose anaerobically and produce methane, ammonia and hydrogen sulphide – all odoriferous and not very useful.

Human pathogens don't like conditions outside the human body, so almost all of them will be dead after a few hours. Only one type of roundworm egg can survive a year-long decomposition period, and even though it is a tiny risk, it is recommended that the compost is used on fruit trees rather than the vegetable garden.

### The Main Benefits
• The solid waste is dealt with on site and doesn't have to be treated with chemicals in sewage farms or end up in waterways.
• Saves water – you don't have to use one resource (pure drinking water) to flush away another (fertilizer).

A campsite with an outdoor compost toilet.

• Organic matter is allowed to go back to the soil where it belongs, improving soil structure and nutrition.

Other Benefits
• No chemical cleaners or bleaches are used in the toilet

• They don't contribute to the sewage sludge that is often dumped in landfill or, more controversially, put onto agricultural land

• As long as the decomposition is aerobic there will be no greenhouse gas emissions

• No electricity needed

• Very low resource use – no pipes are needed to transport waste to a sewage farm, and no truck is needed to remove solid waste

• A clean, simple, hygienic and practical solution

• Cab be integrated for normal domestic use into the bathroom

• Aerobic decomposition breaks down human waste into a safe organic product

• Good for nature and our pockets with no national service bills to pay

• No waste water polluting our land and potentially our drinking water

• Easy to install

• A biological composting toilet providing sound techno-ecological balance that contributes greatly to our peace of mind.

Don't waste urine, even if you do not wish to use a compost toilet. Collect it in a container and throw it onto the compost heap, resulting in an excellent source of nitrates for your garden.

## SEPTIC TANK SEWAGE TREATMENT SYSTEMS

*Septic Tank Sewage Treatment Systems (or septic tank systems) treat sewage at its location rather than transporting it to a sewer or larger treatment system nearby.*

### How They Work
Untreated waste water from a property flows into the septic tank, where the solids separate from the liquids. Some solids, such as soap scum or fat, will float to the top of the tank to form a layer, while heavier solids, such as human and kitchen wastes, settle to the bottom of the tank as sludge. Self-forming bacteria in the tank help the system to 'digest' these solids or sludge. The remaining liquids flow out of the

tank to a land drainage system or drainfield. Baffles built into the tank hold back the floating scum from moving past the outlet of the tank. It is generally recommended that septic tanks be pumped out annually, or the sludge and scum layers be measured at least every year so that solids don't wash out into the soil treatment system. Solids can clog the soil and limit its ability to properly treat the septic tank effluent.

Vent pipes should be fitted to release into the atmosphere any gases that rise from the sludge. Suitable covers, capable of supporting an adult's weight, should always be placed completely over a septic tank and to prevent children/animals from falling into the tank.

These days, commercially manufactured septic tanks, are now available. They are commonly spherical in shape with a narrow shaft at the top joined to a manhole cover at ground level. These tanks have built into them several baffles, which perform the same function as the dip pipes and separate out the heavier solids to the bottom, letting the greases/scum and effluent rise to the top. These types of tanks are most commonly used in the developed world as they can readily and quickly be made, delivered rapidly to site, and easily placed in the ground.

Care should be taken, however, to ensure that these tanks will not rise out

of the ground when they are emptied due to high water tables in the ground!

The effluent from a septic tank still contains about 70 per cent of the polluted matter in the sewage, and hence there is a need for further treatment of the liquid from the tank.

All kinds of septic tank should be fitted by an expert.

## REED BED SEWAGE TREATMENT SYSTEMS
*The reed bed is an attractive way of dealing with houschold effluence in a natural and sustainable way.*

The principle of the treatment of sewage by reed beds is relatively simple. The common reed *(Phragmites australis)* has the ability to transfer oxygen from its leaves, down through its stem, porous speta and rhizomes, and out via its root system into the rhizosphere (root system). As a result of this action, a very high population of micro-organisms occurs in the rhizosphere, with zones of aerobic, anoxic and anaerobic conditions. Therefore, with the waste water moving very slowly and carefully through the mass of reed roots, this liquid can be successfully treated in a manner somewhat similar to conventional biological filter bed systems of sewage treatment.

The reed beds must be located in a sunny position so that the reeds grow

## HARVESTING WATER

This is a process whereby rainwater can be accumulated in containers and used for a variety of purposes. In some cases, rainwater may be the only economical water source available. Rainwater harvesting systems can be simple to construct from inexpensive local materials, and are potentially successful in most habitable locations. Water collected by this method can be harmful to human health, but it can be used for flushing toilets, washing clothes, watering the garden and washing cars; these uses alone halve the amount of water used in a typical home. This water cannot be used for drinking unless a purification system

to their full potential. A four-bedroom house will require a reed bed of approximately 270ft$^2$ (25m$^2$). This is grown in a sealed concrete or brick area. Space will also be required for a holding tank, which will contain sludge, which should be emptied every three years or so.

ABOVE: The common reed has a natural ability to filter out toxins in water and can be used to treat sewage.

RIGHT: A cheap and easy way to harvest rainwater is by installing water butts.

has been installed. Household rainfall catchment systems are appropriate in areas with an average rainfall greater than 7.9in (200mm) per year.

These harvesting systems channel rainwater that falls on to a roof into storage via a system of gutters and pipes. The first flush of rainwater after a dry season should be allowed to go to waste as it will be contaminated with dust, bird droppings, etc. Roof gutters should have a sufficiently deep incline to avoid standing water, and must be strong enough and large enough to carry peak flows. Storage tanks should be covered to prevent mosquitoes from breeding in them and to reduce evaporation losses, contamination and algal growth. Rainwater harvesting systems require regular maintenance and cleaning to keep the system clean and hygienic.

Harvesting rainwater can assure an independent water supply during water restrictions. It is usually of acceptable quality for household needs other than drinking. Running costs are negligible, and they provide water at the point of consumption.

## NATURAL WELLS, BOREHOLES AND SPRINGS

If you are lucky enough to own a natural spring or well on site, make sure you make good use of it. Have the water tested regularly for contamination, however, and you must protect its purity. Natural water sources may be contaminated by pesticides, fertilizers or animal faeces, so be on your guard.

Water boreholes are a modern equivalent to the century-old water well, boreholes being smaller, less intrusive and easier to maintain.

Boreholes are an alternative to a mains water supply, providing you with your own personal and private water supply and giving you the freedom to use it to provide your home with a pure drinking water supply, or as a domestic water supply for garden or farm irrigation. Each country, state or county may have its own rules and regulations regarding boreholes, making it necessary to check these out.

As water passes through the ground and into the water table it

flows through layers of rock and chalk, which act as natural filters. This produces water that is usually far cleaner and purer than that provided by water companies (as anyone who has had their supply analyzed will surely verify).

A borehole, as soo as it has been drilled and equipped, will provide water regardless of climate and independently of any hosepipe ban. You will be able to turn off the supply, coming from your local water company, and put a stop to huge bills landing on your doorstep.

In the long term, a borehole provides a tangible, environmentally friendly and positive selling point when selling a house, which is reflected in the increasing number of people opting to install one.

OPPOSITE: Natural springs can be harnessed to provide fresh drinking water.

ABOVE: Wells and boreholes provide independent water sources for the home.

# CHAPTER EIGHT

# PRESERVING FOODS

### Drying Herbs and Flowers
Fresh herbs, such as thyme, sage and oregano, are often used in large quantities for cooking and a few jars or bunches of them in dried forms make an excellent standby for winter use. The herbs will be at their best just before flowering, but be sure to pick them on a fine morning when the dew on them has evaporated.

Hang the herbs up in bunches in a warm, dry place, which can be out of doors in daytime if the weather is fine, but do expose to full sunlight. The herbs need not be covered, but the bunches can be put into cheesecloth bags to protect them from flies and dust if you prefer.

When the herbs are dry, rub or crush them lightly and store. It is important not to keep them in clear glass bottles or jars, which will cause the flavour to deteriorate.

Seedheads from such plants as fennel are picked when the seeds are ripe and they are dried upside-down. Shake off the seeds from the seedheads when completely dry and store in clearly labelled opaque jars.

Lavender, roses and other flowers can be dried in the same way. Pick the flowers when at a peak of freshness and fragrance, then hang them upside-down. When dry, gently rub off the petals for pot-pourri or leave as they are for winter decoration.

### Drying Fungi
You may discover a cache of field mushrooms large enough to make it

LEFT: Herbs and vegetables hung up to dry.

OPPOSITE ABOVE: Lavender can be dried and used to scent linen, or it can be used sparingly as a flavouring in cooking.

RIGHT: Dried mushrooms can be reconstituted in water before using in risottos and stews.

worthwhile preserving them (assuming you know for sure what they are). While fungi can be successfully frozen, the more traditional way is to dry them, which, as in the case of dried herbs, concentrates the flavour wonderfully.

Pick over the fungi, keeping only the best specimens, and wipe or brush off any earth (do not wash or peel them). Spread them out on aluminium foil and dry them in a very low oven or in the sun until they have assumed the texture of fine leather. Alternatively, thread the mushrooms onto strings and hang them up in a warm, dry place. When dry, store in jars for later use.

## Drying Fruits

You are more likely to have a surplus of fruit than anything else and may wish to preserve it in its 'natural' form for later use as well as making jams, jellies and chutneys. The best fruits to dry are cherries, bilberries and plums.

Sun-drying would be ideal, if you can rely on the weather, but the fruits can also be dried in a low oven. They should be spread out on baking trays, covered with cheese cloth, and will be ready when dry but still pliable. Make sure the storage containers are totally dry and well-sealed to prevent the dried fruit from absorbing moisture and going mouldy. Pick cherries with the stalks on and do not remove pits. When dry, leave for several hours before storing.

Sloes and plums should first be scalded with boiling water to split the skins, then patted dry on kitchen paper, while apples can be peeled, cored, cut in slices and threaded on strings to hang about a warm stove or range, or alternatively oven-dried. To prevent the apples from turning brown, dip the slices in slightly salted water, patting it off with kitchen paper before drying them as above.

RIGHT: Dried fruits are delicious eaten as they are or cooked to produce a winter compote.

OPPOSITE: A satisfying winter store of bottled fruits and vegetables.

## Bottling Fruits and Vegetables

Jars of fruits, vegetables and pickles, kept for winter in rows on pantry shelves, could not be a more homely or satisfying sight, although to a certain extent, especially with the advent of the home freezer, home bottling has become something of a dying art.

If you grow your own produce, however, you will often find yourself with a glut on you hands once autumn arrives, and bottling is the ideal way of dealing with it, for which a supply of thick glass jars with special screw-on lids will be needed. This will only be a one-off expense as they can be re-used year after year.

Bottling works by sterilizing the bottle with its contents, thus killing off all organisms such as yeasts and moulds, and inactivating the enzymes that could lead to spoilage of the bottle contents. A pressure cooker is the safest method of sterilization, and you must follow the instructions for bottling given by the pressure cooker manufacturer.

Fruits, being usually sufficiently acid to prevent the growth of bacteria, are the most suitable for bottling. They should always be of good quality, with all unsound specimens removed. Top and tail as necessary if bottling the fruit whole. Whole fruit, such as currants and plums, must be ripe, but use unripe gooseberries to help retain their texture.

Warm the bottles or jars and pack to the tops with the fruits, pressing them well down. Fill up the jars with hot sugar syrup, allowing room for expansion, and tilt the jars slightly this way and that to expel air bubbles. Screw the lids down firmly, then unscrew a fraction. (The sugar syrup consists of 5oz/150gm of sugar, dissolved in 1 pint/ 600ml of hot water.) Stand jars on the trivet in the pressure cooker, then cook for the time recommended by the manufacturer. Remove from the pressure cooker, then tighten the lids on the jars. Allow to cool before labelling.

Because most vegetables have very low levels of natural acidity, special precautions need to be taken to prevent the growth of dangerous bacteria such as *Clostridium botulinum*. Therefore, increased pressure cooking times are required (see manufacturer's instructions for individual vegetables).

## Nuts

Keep a few nuts in your pantry, but remember that birds and animals rely on them greatly for their survival. Chestnuts and hazel nuts change from the green, milky texture of the young, freshly picked to a later crisp and drier texture.

Make sure nuts for storage are kept away from damp, hung up in nets so that the air can circulate. (The plastic

ABOVE: Nuts should be stored in nets with plenty of air circulating.

OPPOSITE: Nature's bounty preserved in a bottle.

chutneys. For the latter, almost anything goes and you can experiment with any spices or flavourings you like. The general principle of pickle-making is that the character of the fruit or vegetable is preserved, its flavour enhanced by the liquid in which it is stored, which is usually sweetened vinegar or brine. Vinegar is generally a more effective preserver, with brined pickles being intended for more immediate consumption. To be on the safe side, however, you might like to heat-process your jars of pickles for half-an-hour as in bottling fruits.

Nuts can be pickled, the classic being walnuts, but green hazel nuts could also be used. Pickling nuts is a rather more complicated process, but pickling vegetables is relatively easy. The vinegar used must be boiled up with pickling spices (crushed and tied in a piece of cheese cloth) and sugar. Any kind of vinegar can be used and any sugar, with brown sugar, of course, giving a darker colour.

For a crisp pickle, allow the spiced vinegar to cool before pouring it into the jars, otherwise pour it in hot. Some fruits and vegetables need simmering before pickling (i.e., apples or carrots), while others, such as cucumbers, would

net bags in which oranges are sometimes sold are worth keeping for this purpose.

**Pickles, Chutneys, Sauces and Ketchups**

Pickles are slightly more tricky than

ABOVE LEFT: Pickled radishes.

OPPOSITE: Tomato chutney.

be too limp and soft if cooked first. In some recipes you will find that the vinegar needs draining off, re-boiling several times and pouring over again to produce a more positive flavour.

It is important to fill the pickling jars right up and seal to make airtight as vinegar evaporates quickly. Use glass-topped jars or plastic lids, never anything metal, as vinegar and metal react together and cause corrosion.

Chutney-making is much simpler than pickling and has fewer 'processes'. Once you have made a few of them from recipes you will soon be experimenting with your own. Keep a range of spices in your cupboard – coriander seeds, allspice, ginger, chillies, garlic, cloves, peppercorns, nutmeg, mustard seed, mace are all suitable. The vinegar you use will affect the 'character' of your chutney, but any kind – malt, cider distilled or wine – is fine. If you do not have the exact ingredients for a recipe, do not worry. You can always substitute something else and either white or brown sugar will also do.

The fruits or vegetables are boiled up with the spices, sugar and vinegar until a thick mixture is produced. This is transferred to warmed jars, covered and sealed like jam. Most chutneys improve with keeping. With a glut of fruit such as blackberries, it makes a change to use them for chutneys and sauces rather than the usual jams or jellies.

Refreshing fruit sauces make a delicious accompaniment to plain ice cream, custards, milk puddings, etc. Simply boil the fruit with sugar and press it through a sieve. You can flavour with a little liqueur if you like, for instance, crème de menthe or apricot brandy go well with blackberry sauce, though this is not essential. If you like spicy flavours, a little of your favourite spice could go in instead. Taste and experiment at will.

# PRESERVING FOODS

### Jelly-Making

Making jelly is great fun, mainly because it can be conjured up from any fruit to make either a sweet or savoury concoction.

No special equipment is needed, unless you wish to go to the expense of buying a special jelly bag. A clean cotton dishcloth could be used instead, tied up at the four corners, but be sure to wash and rinse it well to remove any dressing before using for the first time.

Wild fruits make good jellies because their flavour is tart and distinctive. Sloes, blackberries, elderberries, rowanberries, crab apples, quinces, haws, bilberries, bullaces are all good, to name but a few. It often pays to add some chopped-up unpeeled and uncored windfall apples to the first boiling to ensure plenty of pectin will ensure a good 'set'.

The principle is simple. Place the fruit and flavourings, if used, in a pan and cover with water. Filtered or bottled water is best as tap water can be quite heavily chlorinated in some areas.

Bring to a boil and simmer until the fruit is quite soft, then place it in the jelly bag or clean cloth (dipped in boiling water, then wrung out) and hang overnight, e.g., from a broom handle, to drip into a bowl. Do not squeeze the bag, if a clear jelly is required, but if you don't mind a slightly cloudy one, then squeeze out as much juice as possible to add to the bowl.

Measure out the juice and to each 1lb (450g) of juice add 1lb of sugar, with rather less sugar if you are making jelly to eat with meat or game. Return to the pan, then bring to a boil, stirring with a wooden or plastic spoon. Boil until the jelly reaches 220°F (105°C) when measured with a jam thermometer (measure in the centre of the pan). If you do not have a thermometer, spoon out a little onto a saucer, cool, then see if it wrinkles when pushed with a finger. Have ready some warmed jars and fill using a ladle. Seal with waxed paper discs and cover.

### Conserves, Jams, Cheeses and Butters

The most common ways of using fruits is in conserves, jams or preserves, and consist simply of fruit and sugar brought to a boil, skimmed and simmered until a setting point is reached, when the jam is put into jars, covered and sealed. It is possible, using mixtures of wild fruits and with the addition of flavourings to achieve some interesting results.

Fruit cheeses and butters are slightly different in that they are sugar and fruit pureés cooked for so long that

crab apples are all candidates for this form of preservation.

## Candied Fruits

Lemons or oranges can be candied and used to decorate cakes. To candy fruits, they should first be simmered in a heavy syrup 1lb (450g) sugar to ½ pint (300ml) water until tender, then taken out and left to dry on a wire tray in a cool oven. Meanwhile, boil up the syrup until thick, cool it a little, then dip the fruit in, using tongs or a fine skewer, until each piece is well-coated. Leave to dry again before dusting with confectioner's sugar and storing between waxed paper sheets in boxes.

## Wine-Making

It would be wise to make a small quantity of wine before investing in expensive equipment if you have never made it before. Making wine is a good way of using up large crops of wild produce, such as blackberries, elderflowers, elderberries, etc., and preserving them in a very acceptable drinkable form. Once 'hooked' on country wine-making, you will no doubt wish to experiment with your

the moisture has largely evaporated. Cheeses have more sugar in them than butters and are firm when cooled, so that they can be cut, rather like thick blancmange. Butters, as the name implies, can be spread. Cheeses were traditionally served with whipped cream and toasted nuts, or with port after dinner. Butters were used as a spread or as a tart filling.

It takes time to make these as the fruit must be simmered slowly for a long time until it is almost dry before the sugar is added. As burning is a hazard the pan must be constantly stirred to prevent this.

Fruit cheeses should be put to set in shallow dishes coated with a little oil. Seal with waxed paper, cover, and keep for several months to allow the flavour to develop. Fruit butters can be put in jars and eaten as soon as you wish, as they are liable to keep less well. Cranberries, bullaces, sloes, quinces,

OPPOSITE: Quince cheese can be cut into slices.

ABOVE LEFT: Candied fruits make a delicious alternative to regular candy.

own recipes, but first consult specialist books on the subject.

You will need a plastic bucket (white is the best), a length of plastic tube, demi-johns for fermentation, and smaller wine bottles for bottling (save up commercial wine bottles), polythene bags and elastic bands, a plastic sieve and wooden spoon, and a cork-driver and corks. Many large drug stores or chemist's shops sell wine-making equipment very cheaply and it will be possible to get most of your requirements, including the additives listed below, from there.

You will need something with which to sterilize your equipment, and many wine-makers use Campden tablets, or you can buy sodium metabisulphite in powdered form. Citric acid is also necessary in some form – buy it as a powder or alternatively use lemons. Pectozyme is required in some recipes to clear the wine, while others stipulate tannin extract (or cold tea) or the addition of dried fruit. Wine yeast is also necessary, either in all-purpose form or specially flavoured, while yeast nutrient is another requirement.

The amount of sugar needed will vary according to whether the wine will be sweet or dry. For a dry wine, 2lbs (1kg) will be sufficient to 1 gallon (5 litres) of water. Use more sugar if a sweet wine is required.

Carefully follow a recipe, although, in general, the method will be as

follows. The day before, start the yeast working by putting it in a bottle half-filled with tepid water, plus a squeeze of lemon juice or a very little citric acid, some sugar and yeast nutrient. Shake well, plug the top with a twist of kitchen paper and leave in a warm place, when the water should become cloudy and with some bubbles on the top, indicating that the yeast has started to work properly.

Prepare the fruit or other ingredients as directed in the recipe. Put the fruit into the bucket. Boil up some water and leave it to cool until tepid. Add the amount given in the recipe to the fruit, juice, etc. in the bucket, plus any additives such as lemons, dried fruit, tannin etc. Then stir in the sugar to dissolve it completely. Finally, add the prepared yeast mixture. Cover the bucket and leave it in a warm place for the recommended time, stirring the liquid well each day.

When the time arrives, first strain the liquid through a cloth into a clean bucket. Next transfer the by-now fermenting liquid into a demijohn, using a jug and funnel, and fit a special 'airlock' in each bottleneck, or fix a plastic bag with a rubber band so that the bag fills with the gases given off as if it were a balloon.

OPPOSITE: A demijohn with fermentation lock during the fermentation process of wine-making.

When fermentation has ceased, and the yeast sediments have settled in the bottom, siphon off the wine into sterilized bottles, being careful not to disturb the sediments. Cork the bottles, using a corking tool, and leave in a cool place for the recommended time, which is usually about six months.

# CHAPTER NINE

# SPINNING

*Using the wool from your own animals can be immensley satisfiying, or you may prefer to sell your fleeces on to professionals.*

Sheep or alpacas, raised for their fleeces, will need to be shorn at the appropriate time.

Spinning is an ancient art in which plant, animal or synthetic fibres are twisted together to form yarn. Plant fibres were probably used first, but animal hair was a close second.

The direction in which the yarn is spun is known as the twist, and yarns are characterized as S-twist or Z-twist, according to the direction of spinning. The tightness of the twist is measured in TPI (twists per inch or turns per inch).

Two or more yarns may be twisted together or plied to form a thicker yarn. Generally, handspun single plies are spun with a Z-twist, and plying with an S-twist.

Yarns consist of two, three, four or more plies, or may be used as singles without plying. Two-ply yarn can also be plied from both ends of one long strand of singles using Andean plying, in which the single is first wound around one hand in a specific manner that allows unwinding from both ends at once without tangling.

Navajo plying is another method of producing a three-ply yarn, in which one strand of singles is looped around itself, in a manner similar to crochet, and the resulting three parallel strands twisted together. This method is often used to keep singles dyed in sequential colours together. Cabled yarns are usually four-ply, made by plying two strands of two-ply yarns together in the direction opposite to the plying direction for the two-ply yarns.

Handspinning is still an important element in many traditional societies. Hobby or small-scale artisan spinners process their own yarns to control specific yarn qualities and produce yarn that is not widely available commercially. Sometimes these yarns are made available to non-spinners online and in local yarn stores. Handspinners may also spin for self-sufficiency, for a feeling of satisfaction or a sense of connection with natural history and the land. They may also take up spinning for its calming, meditative qualities.

Recently, many new spinners have rediscovered this ancient craft,

OPPOSITE FAR LEFT: The direction in which the yarn is spun is called the S-twist and Z-twist.

OPPOSITE CENTRE: Unless you are competent, leave it to a professional to shear your animals.

LEFT: The spinning wheel has changed very little in its design over the centuries.

ABOVE: While similar to sheep's wool, alpaca fleece is warmer, not as prickly, and has no lanolin, which makes it hypoallergenic.

RIGHT: The fleece of a Corridale lamb has a beautiful natural colour of its own.

innovating the process and creating new techniques. From using new dyeing methods, before spinning, to incorporating novelty elements (Christmas garland, eccentric beads, etc.) that would not normally be found

LEFT: Natural fibres and dyed wool.

ABOVE: Wool that has been tightly spun.

OPPOSITE: Spinning bobbins.

in traditional yarns, to creating and employing new techniques. such as coiling, this is a craft that is constantly evolving and shifting.

Besides adding novelty elements, handspinners add variety in much the same way as occurs in machined yarns, i.e., in the fibre, the preparation, the colour, the spinning technique, the direction of the twist, etc. A common misconception is that yarn spun from rolags (carded fibre) may not be as strong, but the strength of a yarn is actually based on the length of hair and the degree of twist. When working with shorter hair, such as that of llama or angora rabbit, the spinner may choose to integrate longer fibres, such as mohair, to prevent yarn breakage. Yarns made of shorter fibres are also given more twist than yarns of longer fibres, and are generally spun using the short-draw technique, used to create worsted fabrics.

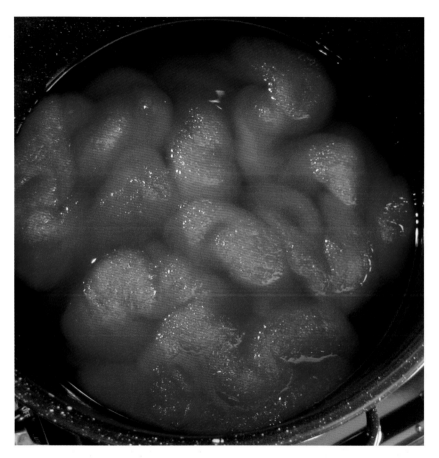

Traditionally, long, fine staple wool was used to create it, but other long fibres are also used today. A woollen yarn, in contrast, is handspun from a rolag or other carded fibre (roving, batts), where the fibres are not as strictly aligned to the yarn created. The woollen yarn thus captures much more air, and makes for a softer and generally bulkier yarn. There are two main techniques to create these different yarns: short-draw creates worsted yarns, and long-draw woollen yarns. Often, a spinner will use a combination of both techniques and thus make a semi-worsted yarn.

Short-draw or worsted yarns are spun from combed roving, sliver or wool top. The spinner keeps his/her hands very close to each other. The fibres are held, fanned out, in one hand, and the other hand pulls a small number from the mass. The twist is kept between the second hand and the wheel. There is never any twist between the two hands.

Long-draw is spun from a carded rolag. The rolag is spun without much stretching of the fibres from the cylindrical configuration. This is done by allowing twist into a short section of the rolag, and then pulling back

The fibre can be dyed at any time, but is often done before carding or after the yarn has been spun.

Wool may be spun before or after washing, although excessive amounts of lanolin may make spinning difficult, especially when using a drop-spindle. Careless washing may cause felting, and when done prior to spinning often leads to unusable wool fibre. The important thing to avoid, when washing wool, is too much agitation and fast temperature changes from hot to cold. Generally, washing is done lock by lock in warm water with dish-soap.

The essential feature of a worsted yarn is straightness of fibre, in that the fibres lie parallel to one another.

LEFT & OPPOSITE: When experimenting with dyes, use fleece that is as white as possible. Dyeing can be done either before or more usually after spinning.

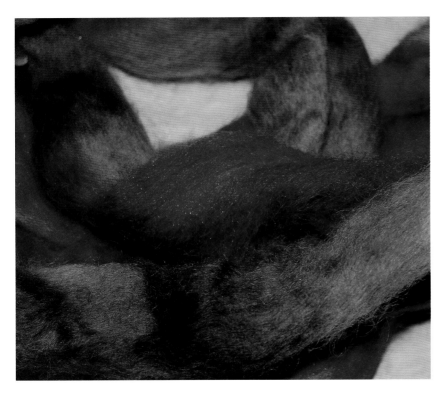

sticky, which makes it harder to spin using the short-draw technique, and almost impossible to spin using the long-draw process. In general, spinners using the long-draw technique do not spin in the grease.

Such spinners generally buy their fibres pre-washed and carded in the form of roving, sliver or batts, which means less work for the spinner, in that they do not have to wash the lanolin out. It also means that they can spin pre-dyed fibre, or blends of fibres, which are difficult to create when the wool is still in the grease. As machine carders cannot cope with wool in the grease, pre-carded yarn is generally not spun in the grease. Some spinners, however, use spray-on lanolin-like products to produce the same effect.

## NATURAL PLANT DYES

Most natural dyes come from plants, the best-known being madder, brazilwood, logwood, weld, woad and indigo. Some natural dyes, such as cochineal, come from insects, while others are from mineral sources. Until the late 1800s, when synthetic dyes came into common use, natural dyes were only available and could easily be used more in the future, being a renewable resource and not dependent on petroleum as are so many modern synthetic dyes.

Plant dyes use no toxic or polluting chemicals, providing alum is used as a

without letting the rolag change position in the hands, until the yarn is the desired thickness. The twist will concentrate in the thinnest part of the roving; thus, when the yarn is pulled, the thicker sections with less twist will tend to thin out. Once the yarn is the desired thickness, enough twist is added to make the yarn strong. Then the yarn is wound onto the bobbin and the process starts again.

Handspinners are divided as to whether it is better to spin wool 'in the grease' (with the lanolin still in it) or after it has been washed. More traditional spinners are more willing to spin in the grease, as it is easier to wash the wool once it is in yarn form. Some spinners may also prefer to spin in the grease as it can allow them to produce finer yarns with more ease. Spinning in the grease covers the spinner's hands with lanolin, thus softening their hands.

Spinning in the grease only works well if the fleece is newly sheared. After several months, the lanolin becomes mordant or fixative, and the organic residue from the dye plants can be put on the compost heap.

Besides using yarns in their natural colours, natural fabric dyes, such as indigo and cochineal, are arguably the only possible colours for dyeing organic textiles. If you enjoy working with wool, either spinning, weaving, felting, knitting or other crafts, sooner or later you will want to dye some of it a different colour. White and natural-coloured fleeces are beautiful in themselves, but

there are times when only bright colours will do. While it is easy to dye your fibres and yarns with chemical dyes it is a lot more fun to collect the plants growing wild in nearby fields and make the dyes for yourself.

## Natural Dyes

Apart from the plants mentioned earlier, good dyes can also be made from the more lowly plants usually to be found in hedgerows and your own backyard, i.e., blueberries, blackberries, red cabbage

(which produce blue); red beet skins (brown); nettles, spinach (green); elderberries, mulberries (purple); yellow onions, dandelion heads (orange); strawberries, cherries, roses (pink); hibiscus, sumac (red), dandelion, marigold, daffodil, goldenrod (yellow); ground coffee beans (lightish brown).

## Making the Dye

Chop the plant material into small pieces, placing them in a large stainless steel pot; then add twice as much water as plant material. Boil for 30–40 minutes, then leave to stand for 24 hours or overnight. Re-boil, then strain the liquid to remove the plant material. If dyeing yarn, tie the skeins in several places and wet thoroughly with water. Place in the dye pot and bring back to a boil. Simmer the yarn, stirring often so that it takes the colour evenly (leaving the yarn to cool overnight in the dye bath will intensify the colour). Rinse the yarn until the water runs clear and hang to dry.

Fleece can be dyed before spinning and does not even have to be washed first. In fact, if you dye unwashed fleece it will be much easier to clean

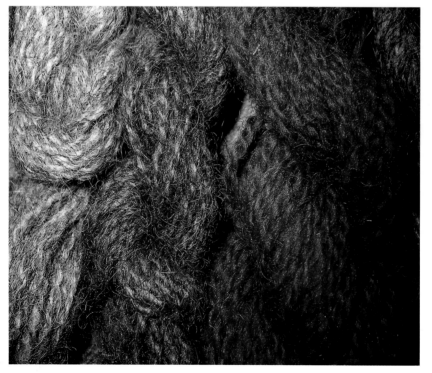

LEFT: Natural dyes tend to produce colours that are far more subtle than synthetic ones.

OPPOSITE: Spinning is growing increasingly popular with people of all ages.

later and the boiling will improve its handling characteristics. Wet the fleece before adding to the dye pot. Pull it apart as for regular scouring and do not put heavily soiled or vegetation-contaminated fleece in the pot. Bring to a boil and simmer for an hour or more. When working with fleece, do not stir it too much or you will felt the fibres. Move the fleece gently in the dye solution using a wooden paddle, pressing and pushing rather than stirring it. Allow to cool in the dye solution and rinse as for yarn. Spread out to dry, preferably outside.

# CHAPTER TEN

# FARMERS' MARKETS

*F*armers' markets consist of individual *vendors, mostly farmers, who set up booths, tables or stands, outdoors or indoors, to sell vegetables, meat products, fruits and sometimes prepared foods and beverages.*

Farmers/producers sell directly to consumers, minimizing profit loss by circumventing the middleman.

• Consumers get to buy direct from the farmer/producer

• Consumers are able to obtain organic fruits and vegetables from certified organic farmers

• Consumers get to enjoy fresh, seasonally-grown food that was produced within a short distance of their homes

• More capital remains in the consumers' community

Farmers' markets are a worldwide phenomenon and reflect their location's culture and economy. Their size ranges from a few stalls to several city blocks. In some cultures, live animals, imported delicacies, unavailable locally, and personal goods and crafts are also sold.

Such markets were commonplace before the Industrial Age but most were replaced in modern times with grocery stores and supermarkets that sell food

OPPOSITE & ABOVE: Farmers' markets have grown popular throughout the world.

produced, packaged and shipped in and from remote places.

Farmers' markets often feature produce grown naturally or organically, meats that are raised humanely on pasture, hand-made farm cheeses, eggs and poultry from free-range fowls, as well as heirloom produce and heritage

breeds of meat and poultry.

Produce found at these markets is renowned for being locally grown and very fresh, the produce having been picked at its peak of flavour, thus preserving the nutritional content. Moreover, since locally grown produce does not have to travel as far to get to

Farmland Trust, sustainable and managed farms conserve soil and clean water and provide habitats for wildlife. Modern farmers' markets, moreover, help maintain important social ties, linking rural and urban populations and even close neighbours in a mutually rewarding exchange.

Farmers' markets are a traditional way of selling agricultural and home-manufactured products, and a weekly market day has long been a part of normal life in villages and town squares throughout the world. A good way for a traveller to sample local foods and learn about local culture is to attend market places, especially when it

your table, the use of fossil fuels is greatly reduced.

It is also believed that farmers' markets help farmers to stay in business in times of austerity while preserving natural resources, while selling direct to the public can secure them higher prices than going through a middleman or supplying supermarkets.

Preservation of farmland is also important for the health of the environment and water supply, particularly in highly developed countries. According to the American

OPPOSITE, ABOVE & RIGHT: Markets are a good place to sell local products such as fruit, vegetables, eggs, honey and even wool.

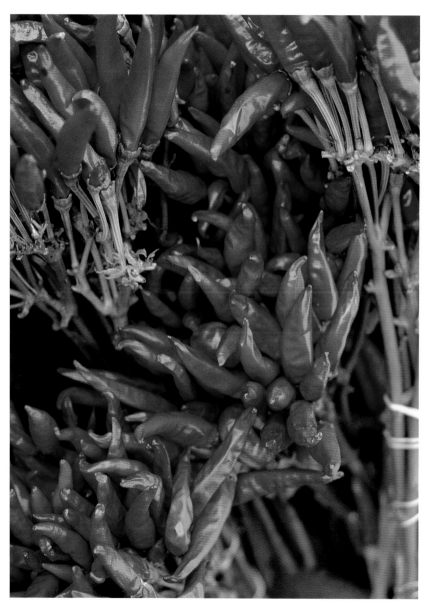

coincides with a festival, such as the fiestas in many towns in Latin America. In France and other European countries, there exist street markets, as well as covered marketplaces, where farmers and purveyors offer their wares. Farmers' markets are even beginning to appear online.

In the United States and Canada, due in part to the increased interest in healthier foods, the desire has been stimulated to preserve local types of cultivars and livestock (some of which may not be up to commercial shipping or yield standards) and an increased understanding of the importance of maintaining small, sustainable farms on the fringe of urban environments has steadily grown. Farmers' markets in the US have grown from 1,755 in 1994 to 4,385 in 2006 to 5,274 in 2009. In New York City, there are 107 such markets in operation, while in the Los Angeles area, 88 farmers' markets exist, many of which sell Hispanic and Asian fare.

New markets are appearing regularly, and existing markets, some well over a century old, are seeing renewed growth in both North America

LEFT: A beautiful display goes a long way to tempt customers to buy.

OPPOSITE: Farmers' markets seem all the more attractive when sited in the centre of a busy and picturesque town.

and Europe. Since the first farmers' market was established in the UK in 1997, the number has grown to over 550 nationwide.

Some markets are carefully managed, with strict rules for pricing, quality and vendor selection, while others are much more relaxed in their criteria. While the usual emphasis is on independent, locally-grown food products, some markets feature co-ops and other purveyors, or allow farmers to purchase some products to re-sell. Sometimes there is fraud and products are mislabelled as organic or locally-grown when they are not. In some cases, fraudulent farmers' markets may sell regular grocery store vegetables, passing them off as the genuine article, which may be sold to unsuspecting tourists.

# CHAPTER ELEVEN

# MILK PRODUCTS

*If you are the proud owner of a cow, goat or even a sheep, it is likely you will be milking it. Dairying is often thought to be complicated, but to make cream, yogurts, soft cheeses and butter are in fact quite simple processes.*

Here is a no-nonsense, stripped-down guide to home dairying and cheese-making that is child's play to follow. And it all begins with milk.

### Milk

Cows' milk is composed of millions of tiny particles of butterfat, on average about 12.5 per cent of the whole, all kept individually in suspension in a solution of water. When processing milk to make butter, yogurt and cheese, all we're doing, in effect, is finding different ways to separate the butterfat from the water and bring them together again in different ways.

It is the quality of the butterfat that determines how good the end product will be. The creamier the milk,

RIGHT & OPPOSITE: Milk is the basis of many delicious products.

# MILK PRODUCTS

the more butterfat it will contain (on average cows' milk contains 66kcal per 3½oz/100gm of whole milk).

The protein, fat, lactose, vitamins and minerals in milk make it one of nature's most nutritionally complete foods. Though most of the bacteria in milk from a healthy cow are harmless or beneficial, the risk of ingesting harmful bacteria, such as E. coli or salmonella, are good reasons to pasteurize milk. Pasteurization destroys potentially harmful bacteria, extending the milk's shelf life. Start with fresh raw milk since pasteurizing it will not improve the milk's freshness or flavour.

BELOW & OPPOSITE: Cream is a delicious component of milk that has many culinary uses.

Pasteurized milk is generally considered safer for drinking, particularly by children, pregnant women, the elderly, and anyone with an impaired immune system. If it is your

242

plan to make certain cultured products from the milk, such as soft cheeses, then pasteurization would also apply.

There are many ways of successfully pasteurizing milk at home. First boil clean, empty milk bottles, submerged in water, for 10 minutes to disinfect them. (Alternatively, milk bottles can be sterilized in an oven preheated to 212°F (100°C) for 20 minutes. Next pour the raw milk into the top of a double boiler, filling the bottom section with water. Bring the raw milk to 145°F (63°C), keeping it at that temperature for at least 30 minutes, stirring constantly to avoid burning. (For a faster method, heat the milk to 165°F (72°C) for at least 15 seconds, stirring constantly.) Use a metal-stem thermometer to monitor the temperature, but do not let it touch the sides of the boiler. Place the top section of the double boiler, holding the heated milk, into a pan of cold or ice water to cool it down rapidly. Continue to stir. Cool the milk until it reaches 40°F (7°C) or below. Pour the pasteurized milk into the sterilized milk bottles. Cover and store in a refrigerator.

## Separating the Cream From Milk

The type of cream is determined by the percentage of fat. There are two ways by which cream can be separated from milk, the easiest being the gravity method. First you will require very fresh cow's or goat's milk (if the milk has been homogenized, you won't be able to separate the cream). Pour the milk into a shallow, flat dish and gravity will, in time, naturally separate sediments and liquids that don't mix. Place the dish in a cool place and allow it to sit for 12 to 24 hours. Use a spoon or ladle to gently collect the cream which has risen to the surface of the dish (only the surface must be skimmed to avoid mixing the cream with the residual milk). Store the cream in a clean, covered container and refrigerate. Cream made using this method has about 25 per cent fat.

The other way is to use a centrifugal cream separator. Pour the milk into the bowl and pass it through the central tubular shaft. Centrifuge the milk. The faster the bowl is spun, the heavier will be the cream. Some cream separators have programme settings that allow the fat content to be set, which typically ranges from 18 to 48 per cent. Turn on the motor and crank. Collect the cream, which the force of spin has caused to separate from the milk, draining it into a separate container. Store the cream in a covered container in the fridge.

## Butter

If heavy cream is what you want, then it should never be over-whipped, otherwise it will turn into butter. If butter is what you want, however, then this is how to proceed. Choose a heavy cream and use it only on or around its

sell-by date, as this makes it easier to work and gives a better yield and improved flavour.

You will need ½ pint (300ml) of cream will a fat content of at least 30 per cent. It is important to leave the cream out overnight at room temperature to allow it to ripen, again improving yield and flavour. Next day, pour the cream into a food mixer and fit the balloon whisk. Start to beat at medium speed, but be prepared to reduce to low as soon as you start to feel and hear the butter forming. It is this agitation that will start breaking down the cream into solids (butter) and liquid (buttermilk), and it should take only a couple of minutes. At this point, turn the food mixer down low and continue for a couple more minutes to make certain all the butter solids have been removed. A little sea salt can be

added if required. The process is complete when the butter has formed around the whisk in one solid mass. Scrape it off and run it under the cold water tap. This will clean the butter by removing any remaining deposits of buttermilk that will lead to spoilage. Place the butter on a board, using two wooden spoons or butter pats to shape and work any remaining buttermilk out of the butter.

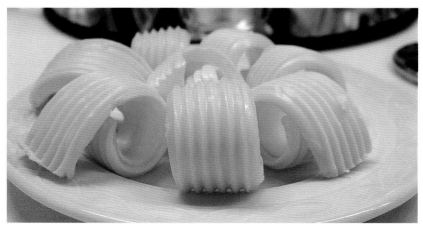

Home-made butter is easy to make and particularly delicious to eat.

## Yogurt

Two teaspoonfuls of live natural yogurt are needed to use as a starter (the trick being to save a little from the last batch you made to create the next) as well as 2 pints (1$^{1}$/8 litres) of milk (skimmed, semi-skimmed or whole; goat's, sheep's or cow's all work well).

Put the milk into a heavy-based saucepan over a low heat and heat to 100–110°F (38–43°C) to kill off any existing bacteria. Pour the milk into a wide-mouthed vacuum flask, stir in the live yogurt, seal, and leave overnight (10–12 hours). In the morning, tip the resulting yogurt into a dish and chill in the fridge for a couple of hours to thicken, when it is ready to eat.

Yogurt can be flavoured, and all fruit, fresh or canned, works well, particularly strawberries, raspberries or blackcurrants. Other flavourings and additions can include honey, nuts, muesli, raisins and sultanas, and, mixed with crushed avocado, it can be used as a dip.

## Curd Cheese

Curd or cottage cheese is a soft cheese that is neither pressed nor matured and retains a high level of moisture in the curd. It can be made with any type of milk, including that taken from goats

Yogurt is easy to make and provides a tasty breakfast combined with fresh fruit and grains.

and sheep; the higher the fat content, the creamier the curd will be. It will be much lower in fat if made with skimmed or semi-skimmed milk, making it popular with people watching their weight.

Pour 4 pints (2$\frac{1}{4}$ litres) of milk into a heavy-based saucepan and bring to a boil, then remove from the heat. Squeeze in the juice of a lemon and stir: the mixture will separate into curds and whey. Line a fine sieve with a muslin cloth, pour the mixture into it and allow the whey to drain off, leaving the curd cheese behind in the sieve. Add a little salt and place in shallow bowl lined with a paper towel. Air dry, stirring occasionally and replacing the paper towel as necessary. The longer you leave it (up to a day), the firmer the cheese will be, when it will be possible to slice it with a knife.

Variation: If a cheese resembling mascarpone is required, replace the milk with heavy cream and maintain the heat for 2 minutes before draining through muslin.

LEFT: Curd cheese, cut unto slices.

RIGHT: Using heavy cream instead of milk will produce a mascarpone-type cheese used in tiramisu, the popular Italian dessert.

# INDEX

**A**

acid rain 8
advice, courses 21, 171
allotments 7, 10, 11, 12–13
  rules and regulations 13
alpacas 166-169, 226
  accommodation 167
  feeding 167, 168
  health and nutrition 168
American Farmland Trust 237
American Livestock Breed
  Conservancy 134
animals
  care of (see individual entries)
  for meat 10
apples 96–97
aubergines (see eggplants)

**B**

balconies and window sills, growing
  crops on 11
barns 30–34, 144
beans
  fava (broad) 58
  green 58
  red (kidney) 58
beds, raised 11, 47, 49
bee-keeping 11, 36, 170–185 (see also
  honey)

aquiring bees 176–177
colonies, inspecting 181
demonstrations (bee-keeping) 171
egg-laying 180
foulbrood 175
hive tools 174
hives
  clearers (escape boards) 176
  feeders 176, 180
  frames 176
  inspection of 179, 180
  positioning of 171
  queen excluders 175
  supers 175
  transferring bees to 178, 179
  types of 174–176
honeycomb 176, 180
  protective clothing 172, 173
  smokers 173, 174
beets (beetroot) 59–60
biomass 8
blackcurrants 90–91
blueberries 89
boreholes 212–213
breed societies 21, 22, 134
British Rare Breeds Survival Trust 134
broccoli 60
brussels sprouts 61
butter-making 243–245

**C**

cabbage
  Savoy 62
  spring 61
  summer 62
  winter 62
capsicums 65–69
carbon footprints 6, 38
carrots 63
cauliflowers 63
celery 64, 65
chemicals, synthetic 6, 9, 44, 189
cherries 98–99
chickens 11, 37, 104–117
  beaks (trimming of) 116, 117
  bedding 108
  claws (trimming of) 117
  cleaning out 108
  dust baths 117
  egg-laying 111–112
  ex-battery 114
  feeding 109–111
  genetic defects 117
  grit, importance of 110
  health 114–117
  housing systems 106–108
  lice and mites 117
  obtaining 112–114
  parasites 116

restrictions 104
roosts 108
tapeworms and roundworms 116
chilies (chillies) 65–69
cloches 16
composting 9, 13, 16, 43, 46, 54, 144
compost toilets 208–210
containers, plant 11
corn (see sweet corn) 79
courgettes (see zucchini)
cows 140–145
barns 30–34, 144
feeding 144, 145
hay 16, 27–28
storing 28
haylage 30
mastitis 145
milking equipment 144
cream-making 243
cucumbers 69
curd or cottage cheese, making 246, 248

D
DEFRA 155
demonstrations (see advice)
double digging 43, 44–45
ducks 118–124
accommodation 118, 121
feeding 121–122

health 123–124

E
eggplants 65–69
energy-saving (see home)

F
farmers' markets 14, 16, 234–239
farming organizations 21
farms
equipment and machinery 18, 30
hobby 13
intensive farming 6
small 16
urban 10, 11, 13
fences and boundaries 34–36
barbed wire 36
gates 36
hedges 35, 43
post-and-rail 36
post-and-wire 36
rivers and streams 36
fertilizers, synthetic 9, 37
fibres, natural 11, 226
fibres, synthetic 226
field shelters 19
finance 10, 18, 20
forage 25
fossil fuels 8, 202, 237

fruit trees (see also individual fruits)
96–103
fruits, soft (se also individual fruits)
88–95

G
gardens, community 10, 12–13
geese 124–127
accommodation 126–127
feeding 124, 126
health 127
global warming 8, 38, 202
goats 146–151
accommodation 148, 149
feeding 149, 151
field shelters 19
health 151
meat breeds 148
milk breeds 148
gooseberries 91–92
grazing 9, 15, 24–26
care of 26
continuous 25
forage 24
overgrazing 16
rotational 25, 26
seasonal 25
greenhouses 14, 19, 42, 50, 51,
52

# INDEX

**H**

handspinning 230, 231
hay 16, 27–28
  storing 28
haylage 30
hedges 43
heirloom produce 55, 235
herbicides 13
herbs 85–87
home energy-saving
  clothes washers 199
  computers 197
  dishwashers 199
  dryers 199
  electric chargers 196
  hot water tanks 201
  lighting 200
  ovens 199
  refrigerators and freezers 196, 198
  temperature, setting 197, 198
  thermostats 198
home, self-sufficiency in the 196–213
honey (and its by-products)
  beeswax 185
  royal jelly 184
  harvesting of 181–184
  uses of 184
horses 21, 36, 158–165
  feeding 163, 164

health 164
heavy breeds 33, 158
hydroelectric power 8, 206, 208

**I**

Indian corn (see sweet corn)
insecticides 189
insulation (of buildings) 11, 200, 201
internet access 20

**L**

land
  change of usage 19
  drainage 36
  family accommodation 19
  grazing 9, 15, 24–26
    care of 26
    continuous 25
    forage 24
    rotational 25, 26
    seasonal 25
  location 20
  management 22–26
  overgrazing 16
  planning permission 19
  purchasing 18, 19
leeks 70
lettuces 71

livestock (see also animals)
  restrictions 13
  rotation of 9

**M**

manure
  animal 11, 16, 43
  green 46
marketing (of produce) 20–21
marrows, vegetable 83–84
milk 240–249
  butter-making 243–245
  butterfat 240, 242
  cream-making 243
  curd or cottage cheese 246, 248
  pasteurization 242, 243 242
  yogurt 246

**N**

nectarines 100

**O**

ocean thermal energy systems 8
onions 72–73
organic movement 8–9, 14

**P**

parsley 87
parsnips 74

peaches 100
pears 101–102
peas 75–76
permaculture 41
pesticides 9, 13
pests 11
pigs 131–139
  accommodation 136
  courses 132
  feeding 138
  health 138–139
  heat stress 135
  restrictions 132
  sunburn 136
  wallows 135, 136
plums 102–103
polyculture 41
polytunnels 14, 16, 19
potatoes 76–77
predators, protection from 35
preserving, home 21, 214–225
  bottling fruits and vegetables 217, 218
  butters (fruit) 222, 223
  candied fruits 223
  catsups (see ketchups)
  cheeses (fruit) 222, 223
  chutneys 220, 221
  drying fruits 216
  drying fungi 214, 215

  drying herbs and flowers 214
  jams 222, 223
  nuts 218, 219 218
  jelly-making 222
  ketchups 220, 221
  pickles 220, 221
  sauces 220, 221
  wine-making 223–225

R
radishes 78
raspberries 92–93
redcurrants 90–91
renewable energy 8, 202, 203. 204, 205,
  206, 208
rhubarb 94
rutabaga 79

S
sewage treatment systems
  reed bed 210, 211
  septic tank 210
sheds 13, 19, 42
sheep 152–157, 226
  buying 152, 154, 155
  feeding 155, 156
  health 156
  legislation 155

shearing 156
silage 16, 29–30
smallholdings 15–16
soil 9, 16
  biodiversity 22
  compaction 23, 47
  contamination 11, 39
  double digging 43, 44–45
  drainage 23
  mulching 45, 46
  no-dig method 46
  nutrients 22
  pests 42
  pH (power of hydrogen) 46, 47
  properties 23
  structure 22
  type 22, 23
solar panels 8, 15, 203
solar power 8, 202–203
spinach 78
spinning 226–233
  Andean plying 226
  dyes, natural plant 231–233
  handspinning 227–229
  Navajo plying 226
  yarns 226-229 226
springs, natural 212–213
squashes 83–84
strawberries 95

# INDEX

swede (see rutabaga)
sweet corn 43, 79–80
sweet potatoes 80–81

T
tomatoes 81–82
transportation, 'food miles' 6, 14, 38
turkeys 128–131
 accommodation 129, 131
 blackhead disease 131
 feeding 131
turnips 82–83

U
US Department of Food and
 Agriculture 155

V
vegetable-growing 38–84
 cloches 16
 crop rotation 38, 41, 42, 43, 45
 greenhouses 14, 19, 42, 50, 51, 52
 growing positions 39–40
 heirloom produce 55, 235
 preparation for 41–47
 beds, raised 11, 47, 49
 sowing and planting 56–57
 tools and equipment 10, 49, 50
veterinary products 18

W
water 19
 boreholes 212–213
 grey 11
 harvesting of 211–212
 restrictions 13
 springs, natural 212–213
 wells, natural 212–213
weeds, eliminating 42, 44, 189
wells, natural 212–213
whitecurrants 90–91
wild foods 11, 186–195
 recognizing 186, 187 186
 using 193–195
 what and when to pick 191–193
 what not to pick 192, 193
 where to look 189
wildlife, encouraging 11, 36–37, 39
windmills 8
wind turbines 8, 15, 204–205
wood-burning stoves 198

Y
yogurt-making 246

Z
zucchini 43, 83–84

# ACKNOWLEDGEMENTS

*The following photographs were supplied through Flickr/Wikimedia Commons/Creative Commons license www.creativecommons.org/GNU Free Documentaion License by courtesy of the following photographers:*

Page 94 right: adactio, Page 49 left: Paul Albertella, Page 205 right: Dominic Alves, Page 235: avlxyz. Page 232: AnnaKika, Page 191: anemoneprojectors, Page 161: Areopagus, Page 79 right: Sandy Austin, Page 50 below: Lisamarie Babik, Page 20: joost j. bakker, Page 82: Darwin Bell, Page 118 right: Biker Jun (falling apart), Page 128 right: Matt Billings, Page 158: Binary Ape, Page 198, 200: Brett Blignaut, Page 196 above: Luther Blissett, Page 16-17: bobolink, Page 7: bobosh_t, Page 249: bob|P-&-S, Page 165: Bruce Bouley, Page 156: Leon Brocard, Page 204: ell Brown, Page 53: Matt Buck, Page 129: Carly & Art, Page 36: Martin Cathrae, Page 219: ccarlstead, Page 22: Jim Champion, Page 52, 199: chatirygirl, Page 101: Jill Clardy, Page 64: clayirving, Page 48: Heather Clayton, Page 92: clotho98, Page 38: colour line, Page 167: Tyler Conklin, Page 136: Dave Crosby, Page 139: Dean (leu), Page 55: dsa66503, Page 137: dullhunk, Page 138: above Lauran Fan, Page 97: fauxto_digit, Page 218: fdecomite, Page 134: Amanda Fletcher, Page 60 left, 81: Andrew Fogg, Page 132; Caroline Ford, Page 118: Tiffa Day, Page 37: dichohecho - Sarah, Page 9 below: DominusVobiscum, Page 144: Lynn Dombrowski, Page 62: Quinn Dombrowski, Page 84 below: DrBacchus, Page 56 below: DrStarbuck, Page 18: Jyle Dupuis, Page 84 above: dyogi, Page 10 above: j feuchter, Page 59 right: David Fisher, Page 8 below, 172: Fishermans daughter, Page 212: John Fowler, Page 91: foxypar4, Page 193 above: Michael Gasperl, Page 78 right: g_kat2, Page 131: Kristie Gianopulos, Page 194 above: Benjamin Gimmel, Page 59 left: Girl Interrupted Eating, Page 87 above: glasseyes view, Page 211 above: gradders52, Page 201: Grayskullduggery, Page 112, 148: Tim Green, Page 173: Peter Grima, Page 147: grongar, Page 8 above: Dave Hamster, Page 174: Don Hankins, Page 141: Kim Hansen, Page 75 right: Haessly Photography, Page 104: Peter Harrison, Page 237 both: heathervescent, Page 19 below: Ken Hawkins, Page 202 right: Allan Henderson, Page 104 below: henskechristine, Page 105: Herbert T, Page 150: Paul A. Hernandez, Page 133: Phoenix Hill, Page 65, 234 above: Hans Hillewaert, Page 59: Larry Hoffman, Page 227 below, 228 left: Emma Jane Hogbin, Page 116: Aaron Holbrough, Page 151: Heather Hopkins, Page 30 paul_houle, Page 178: Colin Howey, Page 221 right: Illusive photography, Page 72 right, 107: ilovebutter, Page 6: Imainjohnson7, Page 231: ingermaaike2, Page 73: Andy Jakeman, Page 226 right: julz91, Page 123: Steven G Johnson, Page 160: jpre86, Page 143: Annie Kavanagh, Page 74: Jeremy Keith, Page 18: Dave Kekish, Page 89 left, 228 left: Jeff Kubiba, Page 109: Liz Lawley, Page 190: Matt Lavin, Page 44: Larry and Linda, Page 197 below: Larsa, Page 153: Keven Law, Page 45: Larry Levine, Page 34: Mark Levisay, Page 164: Steven Lilley, Page 169: Linux Librarian, Page 212 left: Jim Linwood, Page 89 left: Little Blue Hen, Page 80: Llez, Page 115: malerapaso, Page 227 above: Julia Manzerova, Page 120: Matt MacGillivray, Page 76: man vyi, Page 146: Paul Markham, Page 72 below: Martin F, Page 67: Maggie McCain, Page 38: mckaysavage, Page 240: Skånska Matupplevelser, Page 98: Matt McGee, Page 213: Nic McPhee, Page 10 below: mafue, Page 108: Jay & Melissa Malouin, Page 95: marfis75, Page 245 below: David Masters, Page 234 below, 29: Natalie Maynor, Page 14, 113: Will Merydith, Page 87 below: mezuni, Page 4: Andrew Michaels, Page 28: Page 111: Kiwi Mikex, Chad Miller, Page 90 center and right, mwri, Page 124: Mystere Martin, Page 12, 27, 47 61 right, 83 below, 163: net_efekt, Page 189 above: nickodoherty, Page 152: nickton, Page 127 right: noodle snacks, Page 207: nostinkinhedges305. Page 54 right: normanack, Page 23: Carrie Norris, Page 85 above: Oakley Originals, Page 103: OliBac, Page 194: Martin Olsson, Page 239: Ethan Oringel, Page 127 above: owlmonkey, Page 68: oosp, Page 66: Laura Padgett, Page 35 above: Peter Pearson, Page 19 above, 32: Randen Pederson, Page 50 above: peganum, Page 58 right: Bob Peters, Page 56: Photofarmer, Page 79 left: Pin-add, Page 154: Bryn Pinzgauer, Page 58: pizzodisevo, Page 94: polandeze, Page 266 center: Martin Pot, Page 122: photogramma1, Page 100: punkin3.14, Page 211 below: Greg Pye, Page 26: Kevin Rawlins, Page 140: Redjar, Page 35 below: R i c h a r d, Page 117: Ramon Rodriguez, Page 3: Ralf Roletschek, Page 238: George Ruiz, Page 33: Forest Runner, Page 69: rusty.grass, Page 78 left: Tim Sackton, Page 61, 189 below: Andrew Saltmarsh, Page 193 below: Nick Saltmarsh, Page 71: Luis Miguel Bugallo Sanchez, Page 29: Robert Scarth, Page 86: seelensturm, Page 130: Lil Shepherd, Page 9 above: Arkansas ShutterBug, Page 21, 85 below, 135, 159, 214 above: Amanda Slater, Page 51, 229: sleepyneko, Page 192: Phil Sellens, Page 41: slinz0, Page 15: Dwight Sipler, Page 186: Sir Boris, Page 119, 152 above: Hans Splinter, Page 54 left: solylunafamila, Page 220: Adie Reed, Page 205 left: Ryan Somma, Page 40: Southern Foodways Alliance Amy C Evans, Page 155 Steenbergs, Page 114: StevenW, Page 164, 81 left: Dave Stokes, Page 99: Konrad Summers, Page 6, 162: Svadilfari, Page 126 left, 149: Tambako the Jaguar, Page 245 above: taiyofj, Page 49 right: Rachael Tayse, Page 188: The Holy Hand Grenade, Page 196 below: theilr, Page 197 above: Mr Thomas, Page 142: Tony the Misfit, Page 202: totobotteri, Page 191 above: Ross Tucknott, Page 207: United Diversity, Page 203: VeloBusDriver, Page 11: Viewoftheworld, Page 127 below: von.grzanka, Page 248: Lilyana Vynogradova, Page 25: Wackybadger, Page 168: Michael Wade, Page 243: wEnDaLicious, Page 63, 75 left, 90 left, 92, 166: Liz West, Page 230: Natalia Wilson, Page 39: Woodleywonderworks, Page 31: Carl Wycoff, Page 157: xlibber, Page 71: Russell Yarwood, Page 186 above: Steffen Zahn, Page 187: H zell, Page 161: Mark Ziubinski, Page 2, 83 above: ZoopZilla.

# ACKNOWLEDGEMENTS

The following photographs were supplied through © istockphoto, courtesey of the following photographers: Page 224: Gary Adams, Page 110 below: Linda Alstead, Page 185: Gustavo Andrade, Page 222: Nicole Branan, Page 175: Richard Clark, Page 215 above: Mike Dabell, Page 240: DNY59, Page 215 below: Ever, Page 180: Jose Juan Garcia, Page 221: CGissemann, Page 170: Darla Hallmark, Page 171: Peter Engelsted Jonasen, Page 216: Lehner, Page 247: Viktorija Kuprijanova, Page 223: Carina Lochner, Page 185: matka_Wariatka, Page 225: Arpad Nagy-Bagoly, Page 244: milanfoto, Page 246: Antonio Muñoz Palomares, Page 182: proxyminder, Page 179: Derek Thomas, Page 110 above: Iain Sarjeant, Page 241: Elena Schweitzer, Page 242: Gary Sludden, Page 214: Debra Wiseberg, Page 217: YinYang,